AF190498

Rails to Poole Harbour

by
Colin Stone

THE OAKWOOD PRESS

© Oakwood Press & Colin Stone 2007
British Library Cataloguing in Publication Data
A Record for this book is available from the British Library
ISBN 978 0 85361 662 7
First published in 1999
Second Edition 2007
Typeset by Oakwood Graphics.
Repro by PKmediaworks, Cranborne, Dorset.
Printed by Cambrian Printers, Aberystwyth, Ceredigion.

I would like to dedicate this book to my late uncle, William 'Wiggy' Hayne who fired my interest in steam locomotives and railways, and to my late father Ernest 'Ernie' Stone who loved Poole so much.

Above: In February 1977 Poole goods yard has a 'Big ED' class '74' No. 74003 in residence. The locomotive had just brought in the daily freight from Wimborne. Seen in conversation with the guard and shunter is driver Bob Goodfellow, he was a colourful character who came to work in an old ex-Army wrecking vehicle and drove trains in an unofficial uniform of Army greatcoat, bowler hat and wellington boots. *Fred Worth*

Title page: A fine broadside shot of No. 1 *Bonnie Prince Charlie* at the entrance to the coal yard and wharf in August 1954. The rails to New Quay are visible behind the engine.
Ivo Peters courtesy of Julian Peters

Front cover: In this view taken in August 1954 class 'B4' 0-4-0T No. 30093 is seen on Poole Quay. The engine is passing Yeatmans Flour Mill (*left*) propelling two box vans, these were most probably collected in West Quay Road on its journey to the Quay. Moored up on the right is the *Matapan*, a familiar sight in Poole for many years giving pleasure trips around the Harbour. *Ivo Peters, courtesy of Julian Peters*

Rear cover, top: On 2nd January, 2007 class '442' 'Wessex Electric' No. 2412 flashes over Rockley Bridge spanning the outlet from Lytchett Bay, Poole Harbour with a Weymouth-Waterloo service. *Author*

Rear cover, bottom: In 1961, Rebuilt Bullied Pacific No. 34040 *Crewkerne* storms up Parkstone bank with an up train from Weymouth. *Colour-Rail/R.D. White*

Published by The Oakwood Press (Usk), P.O. Box 13, Usk, Mon., NP15 1YS.
E-mail: sales@oakwoodpress.co.uk
Website: www.oakwoodpress.co.uk

Contents

Having arrived at the head of the 10.08 York-Poole service on 20th August, 1966 'Black Five' 4-6-0 No. 45132 hitches a ride to Branksome Carriage Sidings on the rear of the empty coaching stock working. *Colin Caddy*

Poole Harbour.

Reproduced from the 1", 1919 Ordnance Survey Map

Foreword

This study of the railways to Poole Harbour was inspired by two factors. First, the year 1997 saw the 150th anniversary of the arrival of the railway in Poole. Secondly, a local study project about Poole Quay was undertaken by students of Carter Community School of Hamworthy, Poole. This study revealed that most of the students did not know that a railway once ran along Poole Quay and had little knowledge of the railway history aspect of their town's transport system. The author (employed as a school technician) was approached by the then history teacher to supply railway-orientated material for a subsequent school display. From that the author was 'cunningly' led into trying to bring together what known facts existed about the railway on Poole Quay so that a very brief historic outline in small booklet form could then be produced as a reference source for any repetition of the project.

As research progressed it was discovered that several photographs and references had appeared in various publications about the line to Poole Quay. Once collated into one block of text complete with photographs it was decided to include other parts of the Poole railway system, thus a small 30 page booklet was produced and placed into the history faculty library. By various means a copy found its way to certain interested parties and from these persons came a suggestion to expand the theme, coupled with a further suggestion, much to the author's surprise, of publication! After much more research the booklet, like Topsy, just 'growed and growed', therefore this modest offering is the result.

Although the main subject of the booklet is the railway system in the Poole area it may, as was the original intention, be read as a reference source by interested persons other than railway enthusiasts. Therefore local area, place, street and location names are given, this may assist local readers or interested visitors to Poole in identifying certain former railway locations. Thus some railway terms within the text are explained for the layman, and I trust any railway enthusiast reader will not think these sections patronising and bear with the author at the appropriate point.

The book has by its nature a set of lists, tables and numbers included, but, I hope, not to an excess, also hopefully it has struck a balance between historical references and the other lighter, human aspects of the railway system within the Poole area. Finally the booklet may stir some memories for a few old 'Pooleites' or offer to those unfamiliar with the area a small window back in time to the days prior to Poole Town Quay's present 'Fun Fair' status, when it was a proper working quay.

My thanks go to two former members of Carter Community School teaching staff. Reg Stokes, the history teacher who inspired me to take up the pen for this project and Peter Gibbs, technology teacher, for allowing me the time to practice word processing skills and produce the first draft copy. Tony Legg is to be thanked for suppling the material relating to the Creekmoor Light Railway. Thanks also go to Bob Clark, Stephen Green, Mike King, Nick Prior, Mike McClumpha, Robin Moy, Tom Upshall and Michael Day for supplying many items of note.

Thank you to Rhys Abbott and John Barham of the Hamworthy Historical group and Ian Andrews and Brian Elliott of Poole Historical Trust for suggesting and then pushing me forward to publish the work. The staff of Poole

Reference Library and Poole Museum deserve special thanks for their time and patience during my many visits. My gratitude goes to Brian Jackson, Weymouth railway historian, for his generosity in supplying information and photographs he had to hand. Also thank you to Roger Smith and Andrew Kennedy of Oakwood Video Library for their invaluable assistance in supplying old manuscripts which they have uncovered.

Since initial publication many, many people too numerous to mention have supplied, often unsolicited and without reference to financial gain, documents, maps, photographs and, on occasions, personal memories of relevant incidents. Such generosity in this modern day and age is most refreshing and indicative of a certain generation, to all those persons my utmost thanks. The author does not profess to be infallible, therefore any errors are entirely his responsibility and he will be most grateful for any corrections and additional information, especially concerning the South Western Pottery railway extension to Salterns Pier. Finally my sincere thanks go to all at Oakwood Press for their kind assistance and for having the faith originally to publish this work in 1999 and to sanction this latest edition.

Colin Stone
Poole
Dorset

A publicity postcard for Poole-based carriers and local agents for the London & South Western Railway, S.E. Buckley Ltd, taken *circa* 1920 in North Street. The employee chosen to pose for the picture, Mr William Hayne, was the author's great uncle.

Author's Collection

Introduction

Pola, La pole and Pole are three of the past titles of the town of Poole. Poole is a medium size town on the south coast of England which in 1999 had around 140,000 inhabitants. It is situated 105 miles south-west of London on the shores of Europe's largest natural harbour, the second largest in the world, with a shore line of about 70 miles encompassing 10,000 acres (4,000 hectares) of water. Contained within this shoreline are various small islands, the largest, and best known as the birthplace of the Scouting movement, is Brownsea Island where, 100 years ago, in 1907 Lord Baden-Powell held the first Scout camp.

Poole Harbour along with the south coast between Portsmouth and Weymouth benefits from the phenomenon of a double high tide. This unusual tidal flow has a complicated explanation, but basically it is due to the fortuitous geographical position of Poole in relation to hydrographic effects known as a 'standing wave' and a 'nodal point'. These, and possibly the land mass of the Isle of Wight, affect the water flow along the English Channel. It results in water levels receding for 2½ hours after first high tide, levels fall around 2 ft before beginning to rise again for about 8 inches to give a second 'high water' about 3½ hours after the first. Thus Poole harbour sees an almost constant high water level for some 14 hours out of 24 which is a considerably more than the other relatively shallow harbours on the south coast. The harbour can at the present time accommodate vessels of 16 ft (5.5 metres) draught and up to 480 ft (160 metres) length at all tide times and levels. One added benefit is its position in the lee of the Purbeck Hills which afford it shelter from the predominating south-west winds.

Local history notes that by the year 100 BC the area was developing as a trade centre, with Iron Age settlements on Green Island situated within the harbour and in the area of Poole now known as Hamworthy. But the use of the harbour waters, at least 200 years before that time, is documented by the carbon dating to around 295 BC of a 33 ft-long log boat discovered in the harbour mud in 1964. This log boat was, in all probability, used by the local tribes or inhabitants solely within the harbour confines and immediate sea area, possibly as far as Hengistbury Head and what is now known as Christchurch Harbour. It is believed that the Phoenicians visited the area and, until around 50 BC, Christchurch harbour and the Hengistbury settlement were on the main trade route in the area to and from France, this theory being supported by the discovery of very large amounts of amphora pieces used to import, it is thought, wines and fish paste.

What happened in this area around 2,000 years ago can only be assumed from local archaeological finds, but it is thought that Poole Harbour and the Hamworthy peninsular in particular came to prominence in the year AD 43 when the Roman Emperor Claudius mounted an invasion of Britain. Generally it is believed that the Romans used the sheltered waters of the harbour to land at Hamworthy, at first to establish a secure base before striking out to conquer the two local tribes of Belgae in Hampshire and the Durotrigues of Dorset. Then from around 46 AD to 65 AD Hamworthy became a landing spot and supply base for a large Roman fort near Wimborne which housed half a legion (3,000 men), along with other auxiliaries such as archers totalling again about 3,000. This supply was accomplished via a Roman road running from Hamworthy along the west side of Holes Bay then going north to the River Stour and the fort at Wimborne, thus was the harbour first used to transport goods on a regular basis.

The Harbour, Poole

This early 1920s scene on Poole Quay shows the view east with the tramway prominent. On the postcard (postmarked Monday 27th August, 1923) the sender states 'weather stormy'. *Author's Collection*

After the Romans had used the harbour for their initial incursions, it would seem as though its usage slipped back to a relatively low level. The main use of the harbour was for ships to pass through it as an access route to the River Frome and thus reach Wareham; Poole as such did not exist, and is not mentioned in the Domesday book of 1086. Around 787 AD a Viking fleet sailed into the harbour and an army of Danes moved into Wareham, sacking the town four times in the 90-year-period until the year 876. Wareham and Christchurch continued as the main ports in the area until the year 1139, when during the civil war of King Stephen's reign Wareham was virtually destroyed. The silting up of the River Frome and the change to sailing ships instead of oar-driven vessels added to Wareham's decline as a port. Between 1140 and 1145 those ousted from Wareham seem to have retreated down the river to settle on the peninsular we now know as Poole, the first reference to the place name being in 1179 when listed on a roll (list of local inhabitants) as Rogerous de Poles (simply Roger(s) by the Pool), Pool meaning the harbour. The next mention came in 1182 as Pole and in 1224 as La Pole.

In 1248, in return for 70 marks' payment toward Lord of the Manor William Longspee's crusade costs, Poole was awarded 'The Longspee Charter' which freed the town from manorial jurisdiction. This heralded the rise of Poole, and from this point the port became well established. The Port of Poole soon became one of the largest and most prosperous on the south coast of England trading with Europe and North Africa. Indeed the town had become prosperous enough to supply four ships for the siege of Calais, and was the supply and provision base for Edward III's fleet during the Hundred Years' War with France. So much so that in 1377 and again in 1405 the port and town were attacked and partly destroyed by the French. But this was the time of the privateer and the town was avenged by local hero Harry Paye (Old Harry) many times from 1400 to 1407, when he set sail from Poole to attack French ports and ships; on one occasion in 1407 he brought 120 captured ships into Poole Harbour.

The highpoint for Poole and its port - known locally as 'The Golden Age' - existed roughly between the years 1688 to 1815, when the town and port saw a lucrative trade with the Americas including the transport of rice from the Carolinas. But it was its part in the trade with Newfoundland that saw many Poole merchants making fortunes from the mainly fish-based trade. Around 100 or so ships left for the fishing grounds in spring where they spent the summer fishing for the prodigious amounts of cod that once existed in the Grand Banks area.

Some then sailed to the Mediterranean with the dried and salted fish, before returning with wine, fruit, almonds and olive oil in the winter; the remainder of the fleet returned to Poole with some of the salted cod and fish oil along with beaver, seal and fox skins. In general, supplies for the fishing/hunting colonies also went out from Poole: listed as 'exported' were such items as wheat, barley, flour, beer and salt (to preserve the fish), plus clothing, hats, boots and shoes which were all made in Poole thus giving employment to many. This trade was to decrease over the years as the demand for Newfoundland fish declined, also the goods and clothes, etc. supplied from Poole became easier and more cheaply obtained from America as that country became more established.

Poole went into decline as a port and was by the year 1846 seeing use mainly for coastal trade with 64 ships so employed. Some boats called 'hoys' carried passengers as well as freight to such places as Portsmouth, remembered by the public house 'The Portsmouth Hoy' situated on Poole Quay near the former berth whence these boats set sail. However, by 1852 this total of 64 ships had been reduced to just four, their trade lost to the marvel of the Victorian age, railways. The year 1847 had seen the arrival of the railway in Poole.

A view taken in the 1930s of Poole Quay looking west, visible on the right are the rails of Poole Quay Tramway seen leading toward Poole station. *Author's Collection*

Railways of Poole 1920-1966

To Blandford (S&D)

To Ringwood (Castleman's Corkscrew)

To Southampton

To Dorchester

Key

1. Bourne Valley Gasworks
2. Bourne Valley Railway
3. South Western Pottery
4. Poole Gasworks
5. West Bay Military Sidings (1914-1920)
6. Poole goods yard (APC 1960-1975)
7. Hill Richards
8. Creekmoor (ROF)
9. Sykes Pottery
10. Doulton's clay siding (1962)
11. Lytchett Brickworks
12. Dorset Clay Products
13. Kinson Pottery
14. Associated Portland Cement
15. Air Ministry
16. Doulton & Co.
17. Admiralty WWI shipyard
18. J.R. Smith
19. Carter's Pottery
20. J.T. Sydenham
21. Ballast Quay
22. New Quay
23. Lake Clay Works
24. Railway Wharf

MILES

Standard gauge

Narrow gauge

Closed and lifted

N

D. GOULD
5.2007

WIMBORNE

Wimborne Jn – Carter's Siding
Closed 1933
Lake Gates

Carter's Siding
Ex-S&D Shed
Closed 1923

CORFE
MULLEN
HALT

BROADSTONE

CREEKMOOR HALT

Holes Bay Jn

HAMWORTHY
JUNCTION

Hamworthy
Jn Sub Shed

Rockley ¼
Pier

LAKE HALT

HAMWORTHY
GOODS

PARKSTONE

POOLE

Poole Quay
Tramway

BRANKSOME

Branksome Shed

Bournemouth
West Jn

Gasworks Jn

BOURNEMOUTH
CENTRAL

BOURNEMOUTH
WEST

Salterns Pier

Borough Boundary

R.N.C.F.

HOLTON
HEATH

Chapter One

Main Line Routes

The coming of the railways

The 1st June, 1847 was the date that the Southampton to Dorchester Railway opened, the line also being known in those days by the nickname 'Castleman's Corkscrew'. This name came from Charles Castleman, a Wimborne solicitor, and a 'leading light' in the campaign to bring the railway to the area. The 'corkscrew' half of the name referred to the 62 circuitous route miles the line took to cover the actual 48 miles from Southampton to Dorchester.

The line left Southampton going west, before it headed south-west, south and then west again to reach Brockenhurst. It then went north-westerly through Ringwood, curving from there gently round in an arc to head south-westerly through Castleman's home town of Wimborne, and what we now know as Broadstone (but was in 1847 just barren heathland), a final turn to the west taking the line via Wareham to Dorchester. The Southampton to Dorchester Railway existed only for a short time, being absorbed by the London & South Western Railway (LSWR) in 1848

The final destination of the line in several proposals was to have been Exeter via a coast line running west through Bridport and Lyme Regis and possibly Seaton and Sidmouth, etc. One such scheme entitled 'The Exeter, Dorchester, Weymouth Junction Coast Railway' was suggested in 1846 but never came to fruition. Eventually in 1857 when the Great Western Railway opened a line from Yeovil to Weymouth, a connection was made to this line and trains then ran down a jointly-operated stretch of track to Weymouth

At the spot where the line turned west for Wareham, where Hamworthy station now stands (then named Poole Junction), a branch line was constructed; heading south from the main line, it descended gently for two miles to sea level and arrived in Poole at the spot known as Lower Hamworthy (where by coincidence, 1,800 years earlier the Romans had also arrived). Passengers for the town detrained right alongside the waters of the harbour, which must have been a hostile spot on a gale swept, rainy winter's night. They then had to cross the outlet from Holes Bay on the 1835-built road bridge described as 'a rickety affair' which was said to 'squeak, shriek and creak' as a cart passed over it.

Eventually in December 1872 a second branch line was opened from Broadstone, then called New Poole Junction (at the same time Poole Junction was renamed Hamworthy Junction), this line came directly into Poole town at a new station, the site of which is still in use as the present day Poole station. From this 'new' station a street tramway was laid to run via Nile Row, West Quay Road and then along Poole town quay, opening for traffic on 15th June, 1874, thereby giving the wharves and quays of the Port of Poole access to the expanding network of Britain's railways. This expansion locally being eastwards to Bournemouth West in 1874, construction work on this new route necessitated a causeway to be built bisecting Parkstone Bay within Poole

A Beattie 2-4-0 as modified by Adams is seen soon after entering Poole on the former Southampton & Dorchester Railway. It is climbing away from Wimborne at Merley in 1901 having just passed under the Poole to Wimborne road bridge. This section of line passed through Poole Rural District amalgamated into the Borough of Poole in 1933. The Broadstone Permanent Way gang are in view, the gentleman nearest the camera, Jim Cox, was injured when jumping clear of flying debris in the Broadstone accident referred to in the text.

Terry Saunders Collection

The other end of Poole borough on the original Southampton & Dorchester Railway route at Hamworthy Junction *circa* 1880. This picture, one of the earliest known of the Poole railway scene, depicts a Beattie 2-4-0 Well Tank No. 186 standing in the up platform. Also in view are the original station buildings dating from 1847, these were demolished in 1892 during station remodelling. *R.C. Riley/Transport Treasury Collection*

Parkstone station viewed looking west around 1900 with an up LSWR service. Once again the train engine is a Beattie 2-4-0.   *Lens of Sutton*

Harbour. The enclosed area of water eventually gave rise in 1890 to Poole Park boating lake. Further extension came in 1888, from Branksome on through Bournemouth Central to join the original 'Castleman's Corkscrew' at Brockenhurst. Poole's final piece of national railway network to be built was on a second causeway across another harbour backwater called Holes Bay and opened in 1893. This completed a second more southerly through route paralleling 'Castleman's Corkscrew' from Brockenhurst to Hamworthy Junction. Some parts of the 'Corkscrew' still exist between Southampton and Brockenhurst, and Hamworthy and Weymouth, but the section from Brockenhurst via Wimborne to Hamworthy, known to all railwaymen locally as 'The Old Road', was closed to passengers on 4th May, 1964. The section from Brockenhurst to Ringwood closed completely on that date leaving the remainder as freight-only. Progressively over the next 10 years as sections were closed even to freight traffic (as listed on page 17), the track was lifted, leaving finally just the section from Broadstone to Wimborne with a weekday goods train.

In this view an Adams 0-6-0 class '395' goods engine is seen heading an up passenger train *c.* 1905 at Sterte, having just negotiated Holes Bay Junction. The locomotive, No. 501 built in 1885, was one of 50 commandeered by the Government in World War I and sent overseas to the Middle East. It went to Palestine in 1917 but was not used there and was sold in 1929.

B.L. Jackson Collection

A photograph taken *circa* 1910 shows a train for the Somerset & Dorset Joint Railway (S&D) running into the down platform of the 1872-built Poole station headed by an S&D 0-6-0 locomotive.

Lens of Sutton

This view of an up train at Branksome station can be dated between 1900 and 1905. Class '348' 4-4-0 No. 348 was the first of its type built in 1876 to a W.G. Beattie design for express passenger use. It was one of eight rebuilt by Adams in 1888 to the form illustrated and relegated to lighter duties, she was renumbered 0348 in 1900 and withdrawn in 1905.   *B.L. Jackson Collection*

A freight train is seen in Branksome Woods cutting in this April 1932 view. It is crossing from Bournemouth into Poole, the locomotive, 'K10' 4-4-0 No. 136 is in Poole whilst the brake van is still in Hampshire.   *Mark Yarwood/Great Western Trust Collection*

The eastern district of Poole is viewed in this 12th April, 1932 scene. 'King Arthur' class 4-6-0 No. 785 *Sir Mador de la Porte* has just crossed the Bournemouth/Poole and Hampshire/Dorset border with a westbound service for Bournemouth West, and is a on a section of track opened in 1888.   *Mark Yarwcod/Great Western Trust Collection*

Looking west from the same location, a Weymouth-Bournemouth Central train headed by an Adams class 'X2' 4-4-0 No. 587 is seen heading away from Branksome, passing Talbot Heath to the right of picture. This is the source of the Bourne stream which runs into the sea at Bournemouth, one tributary rises behind the gas holder seen on the sky line whilst the second passes under the train. This heath was also the terminating point of the Bourne Valley Pottery tramway.   *Mark Yarwood/ Great Western Trust Collection*

From 5th June, 1966 after complete closure of the Hamworthy to Broadstone (Doultons siding) section, the only access to the remaining portion of the 'Old Road' was via the 1872-built Broadstone to Poole section, the latter losing its passenger service on 5th March, 1966 when the former Somerset and Dorset Joint Railway line - which ran beyond Broadstone to Blandford, Templecombe and Bath - was closed to passenger traffic. From that time the Poole to Broadstone route also became freight-only, serving Ringwood (closed 7th August, 1967), Blandford (S&D) (closed 6th January, 1969), Doulton Siding (near Broadstone closed 1973), West Moors (closed 14th October, 1974) and finally Wimborne. Complete closure came on 2nd May, 1977 when a single box wagon containing Wimborne station office furniture was returned to Poole goods yard from Wimborne behind a class '33' diesel No. 33012. This followed enthusiast 'last rites' on 1st May, when the Lea Valley Railway Club ran three trains comprising diesel locomotive No. 33107 and two 4TC sets from Bournemouth and Poole entitled 'The Corkscrew Shuttle'. The route from Broadstone into Poole is now a road for the majority of its course, whilst part of the trackbed from Broadstone to Hamworthy is in use as a footpath, cycleway and bridleway called 'Castleman's Trailway'.

Railways within the Borough of Poole

After May 1893 when the causeway carrying the railway across Holes Bay came into use linking Poole to Hamworthy Junction, the 1872-built Poole station became a through station on two major routes. As such it was being served by the Bath to Bournemouth West services of the S&D and London to Weymouth trains of the LSWR.

Railways played their part in the Poole area in much the same way as in the rest of Britain with the odd bit of industrial line or siding being grafted on to the national system from time to time. As the surrounding area is largely on a clay strata, not surprisingly most of these were sidings into potteries or brickworks. Indeed the final siding in this respect was opened off the original 1847 route to serve a clay pit close to Broadstone station as late as 1962. This was only four years before closure of the Broadstone to Hamworthy section, although access was retained via part of the old down line as a long siding from Broadstone until 1973.

The accompanying map shows the railway system of Poole and the surrounding area with the borough boundaries indicated, within which lay seven stations (if you include the original Poole station at Hamworthy), one short-lived halt and at one time three locomotive depots, albeit sub-sheds. During the 1950s national rail travel reached a peak, this was a time of dedicated workmen's trains, holiday trains and regular use of trains by the general public. From 1960 a steady decline in rail use began, which perhaps only now is a trend which is being reversed as there seems to be a steady increase in railway passenger usage. Railway fortunes appear to be in the ascendancy again, those who cherish our railway network can only hope that the trend is ongoing. So before looking at the main subject of railway connections to Poole Harbour, an overview of the main line railway system within Poole may be appropriate.

Friday 12th August, 1963 and a quiet spell at Branksome shed. This small sub-shed located in Poole was for many years 'home' for the legendary Somerset & Dorset Railway enginemen and locomotives. *Colin Caddy*

S&DJR 4-4-0 No. 78 sits on Branksome engine shed turntable in the 1920s. This engine, built in 1908, was reboilered in November 1921 and finally withdrawn from service in March 1938. *R.K. Blencowe Collection*

A rail journey from east to west across the Borough of Poole in the early 1960s would have given an observant traveller a view of an almost intact local rail system. Apart from the branch to Lower Hamworthy, the use of an 'Area 11' runabout ticket would have allowed rail exploration of the town. The following description, with updates where appropriate, gives an idea of what could have been seen in 1960 when the steam locomotive still remained supreme.

A rail traveller leaving Bournemouth would cross the boundary into Poole about 1½ miles after leaving Bournemouth station. This point is reached just before leaving one of the pine woods that abound in the area which were the inspiration for the name of the S&D's most prestigious train, 'The Pines Express'. This boundary until 1974 also marked the division between Hampshire and Dorset, trains running out of the cutting that passes through these woods emerge onto a high embankment where a brief view of Talbot Heath is had to the right. The heath is the source of the short and narrow Bourne stream (which gives Bournemouth its name) as it flows into the sea some two or three miles to the traveller's left.

Almost immediately Gasworks Junction and signal box was approached, here a siding with access to the main line at both ends could be seen on the right (up side). At one time coal chutes from this siding served the adjacent Bourne Valley gas works. From below the coal chutes an elevated narrow gauge tramway crossed Coy Pond Road into the production section of the gas works premises, unfortunately there is no record of the motive power used on this short system. If bound for Bournemouth West the train would swing left at the junction to join one of the three sides of a triangle of lines and onto one of two impressive Bourne Valley viaducts.

The line swept round in a 180 degree arc, passing to the right enclosed within a triangle of lines Branksome engine shed. Although nominally listed as a sub-shed of 71B Bournemouth motive power depot, in reality Branksome could until 1958 be deemed a sub-shed of 71H Templecombe which administered the shed's affairs. Five sets of footplatemen were allocated to Branksome for working over the famed Somerset & Dorset Railway, their No. 1 job being to work the renowned 'Pines Express' to and from Bournemouth West to Bath Green Park. Sadly in 1958 the Western Region of British Railways (BR) gained control of most of the S&D, only then did administration come from Bournemouth depot. Closure of Branksome shed came in 1963 but it remained in use as a locomotive servicing point until 1965. Small it might have been, but it was Poole's own motive power depot, so long the home of many a legendary S&D engineman. The route then joined the second side of the triangle, the 1874 extension from Poole into 'The West' at Bournemouth West Junction. From here the line began to descend back into Hampshire and West station, the eastern end of the carriage sheds denoting the county/town boundary.

These sheds still remain as the part of the misleadingly named Bournemouth Traincare depot, as it is in fact in Poole. However, returning to Gasworks Junction to continue our journey westward on the right-hand divergence at the junction, a train would cross the other Bourne Valley viaduct and complete the triangle at Branksome Junction on the approach to the first station within Poole borough, its nameboard proclaiming 'BRANKSOME FOR EASTERN POOLE'. Although the line opened in 1872 the station was not constructed and opened until 1893. As the site is in a shallow cutting the brick-built station buildings situated on the up side are on split levels with entrance, booking hall and small

A view east of Branksome station *circa* 1980, in the distance tracks lead left to Bournemouth Central and right to Bournemouth West. The station on this 1874-built line was not opened until June 1893, the main buildings on the up side are on two levels with the footbridge leading left through the booking office at street level.   *B.L. Jackson Collection*

Branksome signal box in close up on 27th August, 1966. The box, seen in the distance at the east end of Branksome up platform in the picture above, used to control the junction of lines to Bournemouth Central and Bournemouth West until closed on 14th December, 2003, it was demolished at the end of January 2004.   *Colin Caddy*

parcels office at street level. At platform level were staff, lamp and store rooms etc., Branksome signal box is at the London end of this platform. The down side is devoid of major buildings except for a canopy part way along covering a toilet block and small store room at the Poole end.

A discerning eye might have espied a line going off on the right, to the rear of Branksome signal box, this led into Sharp, Jones & Co.'s pottery and connected to their 1½ mile internal system. Leaving Branksome the line begins to descend almost imperceptibly at first for about a mile until St Osmunds Road overbridge marks the spot where the two mile 1 in 60 descent of Parkstone bank begins. A stopping train would begin to brake here, as Poole's second station Parkstone is just a ¼ of a mile down the bank standing on a short easier 1 in 300 section.

This station's nameboard reads 'PARKSTONE FOR SANDBANKS', and relates to Poole's famous beach area, situated a good three miles to the south of the station. Buildings here were also on the up side built out of brick, but with a small wooden parcels office as a separate entity to the rear of the footbridge. Parkstone served an affluent suburb of Poole and as such in the late 1950s/early 1960s the goods office remained busy and still employed two road delivery vehicles in its own right. It also warranted under the up side canopy a larger than average (for a small station) W.H. Smith bookstall; on the down side stood a substantial wooden waiting shelter complete with gent's toilet, while to the rear of this platform was a modest three-road goods yard.

From a departing train a line could be noted running south from the goods yard and disappearing into woods, this led to the South Western Pottery Co. The main line at this point, being high on an embankment, gives a wide panoramic view to the left out over Poole Harbour toward the distant Purbeck hills, but the continuing 1 in 60 descent meant trains were soon at sea level and speeding onto the causeway crossing Parkstone Bay within the harbour.

This picture taken from Sandecotes Road bridge shows a train for Poole and Weymouth with class 'M7' 0-4-4T No. 123 at its head beginning the descent of the 1 in 60 Parkstone bank on 15th June, 1932.   *Mark Yarwood/Great Western Trust Collection*

On 15th June, 1932, an Adams class 'X6' 4-4-0 No. E665 pulls away from Parkstone station and heads up the final section of 1 in 60 of Parkstone bank. The locomotive is hauling a train of ex-LSWR coaches on a service from Salisbury to Bournemouth West. This 1896-built machine had just one year left to go, being withdrawn in June 1933.

Mark Yarwood/Great Western Trust Collection

At the same location some 30 years later, *circa* 1965, rebuilt Bulleid 'West Country' Pacific No. 34044 *Woolacombe* heads toward Bournemouth. *Roger Holmes (Photos from the Fifties)*

This view east, *circa* 1965, shows a BR Standard class '5' 4-6-0 No. 73019 descending Parkstone bank with a freight. The consist of vans suggests it is bound for Weymouth Quay and a consignment of perishables from the Channel Islands.   *Roger Holmes (Photos from the Fifties)*

A 'Hymek' diesel-hydraulic No. D7076 (now preserved on the East Lancashire Railway) approaches Parkstone with a rake of 11 coaches in tow. The date of Sunday 7th June, 1964 indicates an excursion of some kind.   *Colin Caddy*

Parkstone station, 112 miles from London Waterloo, is viewed looking east toward Bournemouth in this March 1963 picture. The wooden parcels shed to the right of the running-in board is already showing signs of disuse with wall boards missing. Part of the down side goods yard is visible right, and the Station Hotel is on the extreme left. *Colin Caddy*

Parkstone station sees BR Standard class '4' 2-6-0 No. 76061 arriving with an up stopping service from Weymouth around 1960. In the background the station goods yard can be seen, whilst the down side platform wooden-construction toilet block is also visible. *Lens of Sutton*

Running light tender first through Parkstone is BR Standard class '4' 2-6-0 No. 76014. Proclaiming 'Parkstone for Sandbanks', the running-in board reference is to the affluent residential area of Poole some three miles south of the station. Sandbanks is also the location of Poole's famous golden sandy beaches.   *Colin Caddy*

From Parkstone station footbridge Ivatt class '2' 2-6-2T No. 41224 is viewed preparing to depart on the 5.00 pm Bournemouth to Dorchester service in August 1965. The main line is seen dropping away towards Poole with the line into the goods yard on the left. The white heap seen by the headshunt pointwork is lime scale brought over from Bournemouth Shed water softening plant and dumped down the embankment side.   *Author*

A photograph taken on the 1 in 60 Parkstone bank some 500 yards south of Parkstone station. Rebuilt Bulleid Pacific No. 34029 *Lundy* romps up the hill with a Weymouth to Bournemouth service.   *A.E. Durrant/Transport Treasury*

Rails across Poole Harbour, coming off the causeway bisecting part of Parkstone Bay is No. 34043 *Combe Martin* with a Weymouth-Waterloo train. The Bulleid 'West Country' class Pacific seen in original condition has had a mile of level track from Poole station to get up speed for the 1 in 60 of Parkstone bank. The climb starts in earnest on the bridge.

A.E. Durrant/Transport Treasury

Immediately off the causeway, the town's gas works and associated sidings occupied a large area south of the line, where at times the Poole yard shunter could be noted inside on a trip freight. At the western end of the site was a small engine shed which housed the system's small four-wheeled industrial diesel shunters (*see Appendix Two*).

Again at this point heavy braking would be taking place as Poole station is entered on a tight 10 chain-curve. In 1960 this curve took the line over two major roads on the level. The first crossed was the High Street and was controlled by the adjacent Poole 'A' signal box. This crossing remains, having been downgraded to a pedestrian crossing in 1977 when the box was demolished and the gates replaced by full lifting barriers. Control of the barriers passed to Poole 'B' signal box. Within yards the second road crossed was Towngate Street (replaced by a bridge in 1971), this was at the time, part of the main A350 through the town and was controlled by a crossing box.

The 10 chain-curve continues right into the station where, due to an old agreement with the local authority, *all* passenger trains were obliged to stop. This agreement, originally forged with the LSWR, concerned the position of Poole station in relation to the extension to Bournemouth West. In return for a station close to the town centre at which all trains would stop, Poole council agreed to allow level crossings of Towngate Street and High Street. This was the preferred option to a slightly more northerly route which could, in all probability, have placed Poole station around a quarter to half a mile further west in the Sterte/Poole goods yard area. This would have been necessary to allow construction of an embankment to gain height to bridge the Longfleet end of the High Street somewhere near the present George Hotel. The agreement requiring all passenger trains to stop was finally rescinded in 1961. Poole station's original main brick buildings complete with small bookstall and toilet block occupied the down side platform. The up side possessed more brick-built toilets, lamp room and a store room all linked by a wooden canopy of varying height, also on this side was the main bookstall.

In addition there was a downside bay platform used for parcels traffic, but it was not signalled for passenger train use. All buildings were swept away in 1969 to allow the Towngate flyover to be built. A replacement, but poor substitute, temporary 'Clasp' building sufficed on the opposite end of the up side platform until 1988 when a new permanent building, also on the up side, was built.

Just beyond the end of the down platform and with two sidings running behind it stood Poole 'B' signal box (still in use). On the up side opposite the box was a substantial 17-road goods yard with large goods shed over one track, all served by two reception sidings. If our 1960 train had been sufficiently long and had pulled well down the platform, a glance back would reveal the rails in the down bay passing through boundary gates into the adjacent street and disappearing between houses, this was the start of Poole (Town) Quay tramway. On leaving this 1872-built station past the goods yard, complete with resident shunter,* Holes Bay Junction was reached. This is the point where that last piece of railway to be built in the area veers off to the left on another causeway around to Hamworthy Junction, crossing that part of the harbour known as Holes Bay.

---

* In the 1950s and early 1960s class 'M7' 0-4-4Ts, Nos. 30112, 30318 or 30324 were the most regular performers of this duty until they were replaced by 204 hp (later class '04') diesel shunters.

'M7' class 0-4-4T No. 30112 leaves Poole and crosses Parkstone Bay causeway with a lengthy train. However a plume of steam at the rear indicates a banker for Parkstone bank, while the position of the sun suggests early morning and that the train is empty coaching stock from either Hamworthy or Broadstone. This in turn suggests it is bound for Bournemouth West with the train engine on the rear for a 'right way round' departure later in the morning. The chap bait digging or cockling is oblivious to the proceedings, sadly those pastimes are no longer possible here as the area was filled in within a few years.   *A.E. Durrant/Transport Treasury*

Ex-LMS class '2P' 4-4-0 No. 40564 approaches Poole station with the 5.18 pm Bournemouth West to Templecombe service on 23rd May, 1953. The train is running past Poole gas works and its engine shed (*right*), this housed some small standard gauge four-wheeled petrol shunters.   *R. Gosling*

Poole is entered on a 10 chain-curve and crossed two roads on the level, the first, and still remaining, crosses the High Street. It is seen here in 1977 with its guardian signal box designated Poole 'A', formerly 'Poole East' shortly before it was demolished and the gates replaced by full lifting barriers controlled by Poole 'B' signal box via CCTV.   *Dr J. Boudreau*

From the same vantage point on the High Street footbridge 'Lord Nelson' class 4-6-0 No. 30861 *Lord Anson* is seen leaving with the 4.40 pm Weymouth to Bournemouth train on 23rd May, 1953.   *R. Gosling*

Poole on 15th May, 1964 and a view of Towngate Street level crossing looking toward the Station Hotel and showing the crossing box (*left*) with the former station master's house behind.

H.C. Casserley

A close up view of Towngate Street level crossing box taken in April 1970.   *Colin Caddy*

On 9th April, 1967 a BRC&W type '3' 'Crompton' No. D6552 (now preserved at Swanage Railway) arrives at Poole past Towngate Street crossing box with a 4TC set. This was in the period just prior to the end of steam when certain trains were being worked by the new order. The roof of Poole 'A' signal box is visible above the third coach. On a personal note, the author was employed in the factory in the background (*right*) and on many occasions work came second to train watching. *Colin Caddy*

The second road crossed by the railway on entry to Poole was Towngate Street seen here with BR Standard class '4' 2-6-0 No. 76011 passing over it. In the distance Poole High Street and Poole 'A' box can be seen; the date is 5th March, 1966, the last day of S&D services, and the train is the 12.23 pm Templecombe to Bournemouth. *Author*

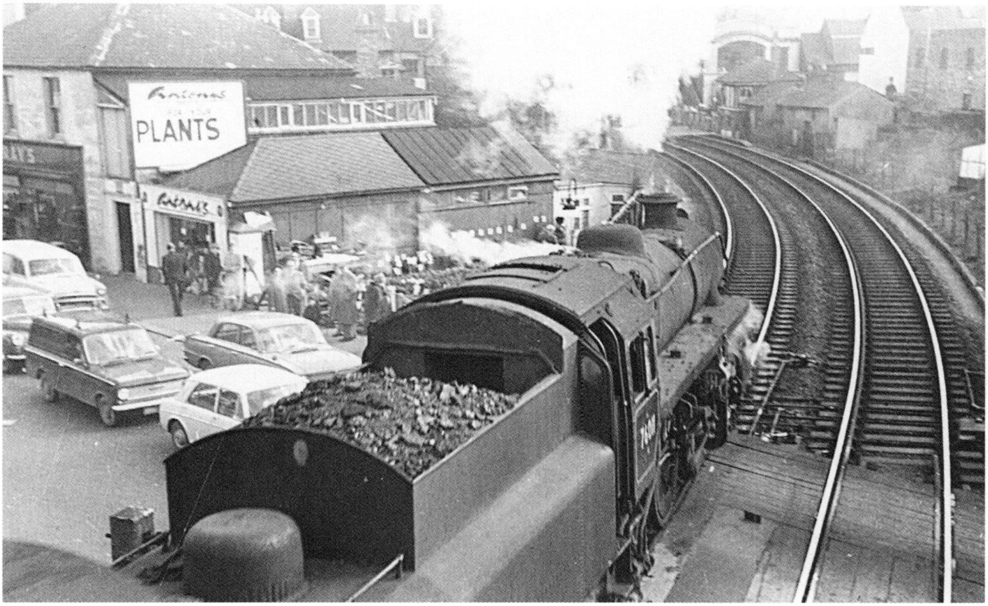

Looking west, Poole station down platform is visible behind rebuilt 'West Country' class 4-6-2 No. 34095 *Brentor* seen departing across Towngate Street on the 10.13 am Weymouth to Bournemouth on the penultimate day of Southern steam operation, 8th July, 1967. As part of the, latterly busy, A350 road, Towngate street crossing was replaced by a bridge in 1971.   *Author*

Setting out over Towngate Street on 10th November, 1953 is '3F' class 0-6-0 No. 43356 with a train off the Somerset and Dorset Railway.   *Colin Caddy*

Drummond class '700' 0-6-0 No. E691 rolls a short freight into the 1872-built Poole station and has the Bournemouth 'sludge carrier' tender in tow, indicating a visit to Parkstone goods yard has been made for discharging purposes, 17th August 1932. *R.W. Kidner*

A former Midland Railway class '2P' 4-4-0 No. 40568 sits in Poole station with safety valves sizzling ready for 'the off' with an S&D train for Bournemouth West in 1955. *Colin Caddy*

Poole station looking west, taken from the footbridge on 1st June, 1953, showing the varying heights of the canopy. A push-pull fitted class 'M7' 0-4-4T No. 30111 is seen propelling the 5.00 pm Bournemouth Central-Swanage 'workmen's train'.   *R. Gosling*

A second view of Poole station looking west; this station was constructed in 1872 and replaced the 1847-vintage station at Lower Hamworthy as Poole's main station.   *Lens of Sutton*

Poole station looking east and a train for the S&D line headed by a class '2P' 4-4-0 rolls in for its mandatory Poole stop. This view shows the severity of the 10 chain-curve that exists through Poole station. *Lens of Sutton*

An S&D train, viewed shortly after nationalisation, is seen with ex-LMS class '2P' No. 40601 in charge. To the right is the down bay platform which was for parcels/goods use only but even this was restricted as the track also provided access to Poole Quay Tramway, seen diverging to the right. *Mark Yarwood/Great Western Trust Collection*

Poole's 1872 station is seen in 1950, 'M7' class 0-4-4T No 30028 stands with a Bournemouth West-Brockenhurst via Ringwood train. Note that two years after nationalisation the locomotive has not received a BR emblem on the side tanks and is also devoid of a smokebox door shed allocation plate.   *R.K. Blencowe Collection*

BRC&W class '33' No. 33032 passes through Poole on 20th July, 1978 with a down freight.
                                                                                    Colin Caddy

To facilitate the construction of Towngate bridge, seen in this photograph, all of the 1872-built station buildings were demolished in 1969 leaving the town ill-served for nearly 20 years by this inelegant 'Clasp' structure positioned on the up side platform.   *Dr J. Boudreau*

A 1970s view looking west toward Poole 'B' signal box (until 1949 Poole West box). In view are a class '47' on an inter-Regional train, a class '33' on a Waterloo-Weymouth train, a Hants & Dorset bus heading up Sterte road and, partially hidden in the goods yard, a 350 hp diesel-electric shunter.   *Dr J. Boudreau*

Hand in hand with the plans to electrify the line from Branksome to Weymouth came the announcement that Poole would gain a new station buildings. In this January 1988 view the construction work is well under way with the arched roof sections being installed.   *Author*

A view of Poole station 19 years later in April 2007, now new plans will see these buildings demolished and a replacement set of station amenities incorporated into a massive redevelopment encompassing the old goods yard site.   *Author*

A ground level view of the 1988 station buildings looking west as one of the new order on the Weymouth line, class '444' unit No. 444008, runs in with the 12.48 Weymouth-Waterloo, 29th April, 2007.   *Author*

The view east on 29th April, 2007, on this occasion one of the German-built 'Desiro' units, nicknamed 'Arkwright's'. No. 444031 forms the 09.39 Bournemouth-Weymouth service.   *Author*

One week before the end of Southern Region steam and rebuilt Bulleid 'West Country' class Pacific No. 34037 *Clovelly* runs non-stop through Poole with empty coaching stock on 2nd July, 1967. One week later the train engine was an electro-diesel. Note the long, arched supports for the down platform gas lamps and tannoy speakers spanning the down bay, also compare this picture with that on page 39 (top).   *Author*

One of the Urie 'King Arthur' 'N15s' fitted with a multiple jet blast pipe and large diameter chimney by O.V.S. Bulleid, No. 30737 *King Uther*, runs in to Poole with two ex-LSWR non-corridor carriages on an up evening service in 1950. Close examination of the picture reveals a 'B4' class 0-4-0T and two box vans in the down bay and an 'M7' class 0-4-4T on yard shunting duties under the water tank in the background.   *R.K. Blencowe Collection*

'The very last one' at 9.25 pm on the 9th July, 1967; having collected two vans from the down bay BR Standard class '3' 2-6-0 No. 77014 prepares to leave Poole with the 8.50 pm Bournemouth to Weymouth van train. This was the very last steam-hauled British Railways revenue earning train to pass through Poole and the last to run on the Southern Region. *Author*

Seen in Poole yard is Maunsell 'Q' class 0-6-0 No. 30546, the picture dates to the time when the 'M7' 0-4-4Ts were almost extinct and their shunting duties were being undertaken by 'Qs'. No doubt their steam reversing gear was deemed an asset for the task. From the smokebox graffiti someone seems to have enjoyed Beatles music and the radio programme Band Wagon!
Alec Swain/Transport Treasury

Poole goods yard viewed from Towngate bridge in the 1970s. Prominent is the Blue Circle cement terminal served by trains of Presflo wagons from Westbury. In the background a Stratford-based class '47' runs-round the empty coaching stock of an inter-Regional train bound for the North of England.   *Dr J. Boudreau*

A picture from a similar position in April 2007 show that the yard has been decimated. The two remaining sidings, one of which is electrified, see occasional use to stable failed electric multiple units or engineers' trains. In a planned redevelopment scheme the sidings are due to be repositioned parallel to the main line and the yard obliterated under flats, retail outlets and a hotel.   *Author*

In the Autumn of 1965 Bulleid 'West Country' class Pacific No. 34041 *Wilton* leaves Poole past mile post 114 with an afternoon Bournemouth-Weymouth service. To the left of the engine is the goods yard water tower, its other use was as a vantage point for footplate crews to watch football and speedway in the adjacent Poole stadium, that is until the night a fireman excitedly viewing a race, fell in! *Author*

Class '33' No. 33113 heads the 08.35 Waterloo-Weymouth service towards Hamworthy on 19th Janaury, 1985 after an overnight fall of snow. Class '33s' and '4TCs' were the mainstay of services through Poole prior to electrification. *Author*

BRC&W type '3' No. D6526 runs past Sterte and into Poole with the 16.00 Weymouth Quay-Waterloo 'Channel Island Boat Train' in 1968. Later classified as class '33' No. 33017, the engine met its end at Vic Berry's scrap yard in Leicester in 1990.   *Author*

The western approach to Poole is viewed again on 24th August, 1963 and can be compared with the 1905 view on page 14 where the only major change has been the addition in 1941 of two reception sidings for Poole goods yard. The train, hauled by BR Standard class '4' 2-6-0 No. 76005, is the 12.16 pm Templecombe to Bournemouth via Salisbury.   *Roy Panting*

The right-hand tracks headed in a northerly direction on the level with the Holes Bay backwater lapping against its left flank, soon a gentle 1 in 400 climb began toward Poole's fourth and 'youngest' station, Creekmoor Halt. The run in had connections into sidings, left for Sykes Pottery Co., and on the right serving a Royal Ordnance Factory (ROF) which had opened in 1941. Until closure of the rail system in 1959 the ROF internal sidings were shunted by an Avonside 0-4-0ST (Works No. 1976) built in 1925. This locomotive was already 'a local' before coming to Creekmoor having worked at the Royal Naval Cordite Factory (RNCF) Holton Heath a mere seven miles away. She was transferred from the RNCF in 1950 and replaced the engine brought new to the ROF works when it opened in 1941. The original locomotive, Peckett Works No. 2012/41, was moved on to ROF, Llanishen, Cardiff; eventually the Peckett found her way into preservation. This former Poole resident spent some time as a 'gate guardian' at the late Reverend 'Teddy' Boston's Cadeby Rectory Railway in Leicestershire. With the eventual disposal of the Cadeby rolling stock in 2006, the engine was moved to Hollycombe Steam Museum, Sussex.

Creekmoor was opened by the Southern Railway in June 1933 to serve the growing Creekmoor and Waterloo communities. Originally the platforms were only long enough for two or three coaches, and constructed from old sleepers. However, to facilitate the workers of the then-new ROF factory the platforms were extended in World War II, and the halt became a typical Southern 'concrete kit' complete with all the concrete extras of fence panels and lamp posts, etc. As a wartime economy a footbridge was not provided, and although the sleeper decking was removed, the original waiting shelters of corrugated metal and wooden construction were retained and remained until closure of the halt in 1966. A concrete footbridge was added at a later date after the war.

Leaving Creekmoor and still climbing, but now at 1 in 75, the line curved round to run parallel with another line coming in at higher level on our left, this was the old original route to Hamworthy and Dorchester. The two lines then converged at Broadstone, our fifth Poole station and in 1960 on its sixth title:

1. 1872 New Poole Junction
2. 1876 Poole Junction
3. 1883 Poole Junction & Broadstone

4. 1887 Broadstone & New Poole Junction
5. 1888 Broadstone Junction
6. 1929 Broadstone

As four routes converged here this made Broadstone the largest in size of Poole's stations with four platform faces, Nos. 3 and 4 serving the original route to Hamworthy, Nos. 1 and 2 the later direct line into Poole, all being linked by a covered footbridge. Substantial brick buildings stood on the island platform (2 & 3), but a wooden construction sufficed for the entrance buildings on platform 1. Part of this structure survives reconstructed at Medstead & Four Marks station on the Mid-Hants Railway.

To continue our imaginary rail journey across Poole, there were from Broadstone three remaining choices of route, the one with least route miles in

Holes Bay Junction, viewed on 7th May, 1967, has BR Standard class '4' 2-6-4T No. 80011 passing over it coming in off the 1893-built causeway route from Hamworthy Junction. The right-hand tracks are the 1872-built line to Creekmoor and Broadstone. A signal box, closed on 28th October, 1934, once stood in the 'vee' on the site of the permanent way huts, whilst Longfleet military sidings were laid in 1918 on the site of the industrial units on the right.

R.K. Blencowe Collection

Passing Holes Bay Junction on Sunday 19th April, 1970 and taking the Broadstone line is BRC&W type '3' No. D6554. It is heading a materials recovery train to Bailey Gate which at the time was the current railhead for the demolition of the closed Somerset & Dorset Railway. Later to become class '33' No 33036, the locomotive met its end when it derailed down an embankment at Mottingham, Kent in 1979.   *Author*

Left: An ex-Southampton docks 275 hp diesel-shunter built by Ruston & Hornsby approaches Holes Bay Junction point in 1976 with a trip freight from Hamworthy Goods to Poole Yard. The Broadstone line, leading off right, had been singled in October 1970 when physical control of the junction transferred from Poole 'B' signal box to the ground frame seen in picture.

Jeff Anderson

Below: A view looking south from Fleetsbridge shows the 1893-built causeway from Holes Bay Junction to Hamworthy Junction crossing Holes Bay; in the middle distance, Poole power station (demolished in 1994) dominates the skyline. Running alongside Holes Bay on the 1872 Broadstone to Poole route is rebuilt Bulleid Pacific No. 34045 *Ottery St Mary* heading the 12.26 pm Bournemouth to Brockenhurst service, in lieu of the usual tank engine.

Roy Panting

Running alongside Holes Bay (*right*) and approaching Fleets Bridge is Bulleid Pacific No. 34054
Lord Beaverbrook in original condition heading a lengthy train for the Salisbury line *circa* 1958.
Colin Caddy

An unidentified BR Standard class '4' '76XXX' 2-6-0 is caught on camera *circa* 1963 running into
Creekmoor Halt with a Bournemouth West-Brockenhurst service. Just visible through the mist
on the right is Sykes Pottery/Brick works, their private siding can be seen behind the platform.
Colin Caddy

Two views of Creekmoor c.1955. *Above:* General view looking south towards Poole. *Below:* This small wooden building served as the ticket office. After closure of the line the hut found further use on the Creekmoor Light Railway (*see Appendix Four*). *(Both) S. Drew*

Seen soon after leaving Creekmoor in the early 1950s are two of Drummonds 'T9' class 4-4-0s, No. 30712 leads a sister engine of the wide splasher '303XX' series at the head of the 7.42 am Bournemouth Central to Salisbury train. They are beginning the 1 in 75 climb towards Broadstone and coming round to run parallel with the Broadstone to Hamworthy Junction line.
John Sansom

This view looks south from Broadstone on 28th March, 1965 and shows BR Standard class '5' 4-6-0 No. 73022 with a Southern Counties Touring Society special the 'Southern Wanderer' coming up the 1 in 75 from Poole and Creekmoor. To the right is the former Southampton and Dorchester route to Hamworthy Junction. Part of the former up line is in use as a coaching stock storage siding.
Colin Caddy

Broadstone station viewed on 22nd September, 1963 looking east. The 1847 Southampton and Dorchester route is seen on the left heading into the distance straight ahead towards Wimborne. The 1872 line to Poole is on the right; note the overall roof on the footbridge. *Colin Caddy*

Broadstone station looking west down the line toward Creekmoor and Poole. By the time of this photograph, 21st May, 1966, the station had been closed to passengers for two months. The train running into the station headed by BR Standard class '3' 2-6-0 No. 77014 is an enthusiasts' special heading for Blandford on the remaining freight-only stub of the Somerset & Dorset line. *Author*

A once familiar sight in Dorset on the Swanage branch and on Bournemouth West to Brockenhurst services were the 'push-pull' trains worked by the venerable Victorian-design class 'M7' 0-4-4 tank engines. In this 13th May, 1961 view No. 30108 pauses at Broadstone with a train for Bournemouth West.   *Colin Caddy*

Broadstone signal box on 2nd May, 1965. Note on the left by the balcony the Whittaker token apparatus for the Somerset and Dorset single line section to Corfe Mullen.   *Colin Caddy*

Thundering up the 1 in 80 from Corfe Mullen Junction on 8th September, 1962 with the last 'Pines Express' to traverse the Somerset & Dorset Railway is the last steam locomotive to be built for British Railways, class '9F' 2-10-0 No. 92220 *Evening Star*. The train is just entering Poole on the 'Corfe Mullen cut-off' constructed in 1885 to avoid reversal at Wimborne. *Peter Dyson/Author's Collection*

the borough was the S&D's 1885-built spur, this single line branched off left and northwards to climb away at 1 in 97. It then descended at 1 in 80 toward Corfe Mullen Halt (opened 1928, closed 1956), at 1½ miles distance from Broadstone and just a few hundred yards short of the halt the line passed over the town boundary.

If taking the right-hand tracks at the junction with the S&D the traveller would be traversing the 1847 original Southampton & Dorchester line heading east for Wimborne, this line skirted woodland before making a gentle descent to Oakley level crossing. Just past this point was the former Wimborne Junction, which from 1860 was the connection with the Dorset Central Railway but from 1863 with the newly-formed S&D. At this junction there was once an S&D locomotive shed, closed in 1923, the junction ceased to be in 1933 when the section to Carter's siding was closed and lifted, although until 1953 two sidings remained controlled by a ground frame. This closure was the first loss of route mileage within Poole, as around a mile of the line lay within the borough, leaving the town at a point known as Lake gates. A short distance from the junction site the River Stour two miles from Broadstone marked the town boundary, across the river bridge and within sight, Wimborne station was but a few hundred yards away. The Southampton and Dorchester company had intended to build Wimborne station on the Canford bank of the River Stour at the point later marked by the Somerset & Dorset engine shed. This was to have been for the convenience of Sir John and Lady Charlotte Guest, the then owners of the Canford Estate, who had given permission for the railway to cross estate land. But the good folk of Wimborne protested, both they and the LSWR favoured a position on the other side of the river nearer the town centre.

Ex-Southern Railway 'Battle of Britain' class Pacific No. 34051 *Winston Churchill* heading a train off the line from Salisbury (via Wimborne) is seen at Merley climbing toward Broadstone in 1963.   *Colin Caddy*

Southern Railway-built 'Q' class 0-6-0 No. 30542 chunters away from Wimborne past Oakley Crossing toward Broadstone. Although the headcode indicates a Southampton/Brockenhurst to Weymouth train it is suspected that this is in fact a Salisbury to Bournemouth West train.

Colin Caddy

Oakley Crossing at Merley on the outskirts of Poole sees an original condition Bulleid Pacific No. 34044 *Woolacombe* passing over it. Once again an apparent shortage of head code discs clouds the identity of the train, but a Salisbury to Bournemouth West train is most probable?   *Colin Caddy*

When the Guests gave their consent to the railway there was a strict proviso that if the railway were to cross their private drive, any overbridge should be in keeping with the main house. This did indeed become the case, therefore in 1846 the railway company employed London architect Sir John Barry to design a bridge to match the Victorian Gothic style of the manor house. This bridge was thought by many to be one of the most ornate railway bridges in Britain. As befits such a grand structure, high quality stone known as 'Ham Stone' was brought 45 miles by road from a quarry near Yeovil for its construction. Although the railway has long gone the bridge is still in existence, known as the 'Lady Wimborne Bridge' it is now in the care of Poole Borough Council. No longer crossed by the 'Castleman's Corkscrew', a footpath and cycleway somewhat cynically known as 'Castleman's Trailway' passes over it, whilst the old Canford Manor driveway passing beneath is now Public Footpath No. 90. With the council's blessing, a small group of persons (mainly members of Wimborne Railway Society) known as 'The Friends of Lady Wimborne's Bridge' organize regular working parties to help maintain the bridge and keep the surrounding area clean and tidy. Had the site at Canford been selected for Wimborne station it would have placed it in what became Poole Borough, thus it would have been the eighth station in Poole.

Returning to Broadstone, although various derailments have occurred within the Poole area over the years, Broadstone was the scene of the only fatal railway accident in the town. On 23rd December, 1890 a class '273' 0-6-0 freight locomotive No. 290 (later re-numbered 351A), built 1873 in Manchester by Beyer, Peacock, overran a red signal on the line from Wimborne. The freight locomotive which was running 'light engine' stopped after the footplate crew heard a shouted warning, but alas it was now in the path of a train correctly signalled coming in off the S&D route. This train hauled by S&D Johnson 0-4-4 tank engine No. 54, built in 1884 by Vulcan Foundry, ran into the stationary engine, the force of the collision doing considerable damage to both locomotives

Simply listed as Bridge No. 77 by the LSWR that non-descript title hides the ornate construction of what is known locally as 'Lady Wimborne's Bridge'. Built to cross a private drive to Canford Manor, its ornate construction by the Southampton & Dorchester Railway was at the insistence of the Lord of the Manor.

Peter (Hussey) Smith

and causing the coaches of the passenger train to telescope. Unfortunately one lady passenger died and three others were seriously injured. The crew of the freight engine were arrested and charged with manslaughter, the charge against fireman Albert Stone later being dropped. The driver, William Squires, duly appeared at Dorchester assize court in February 1891, but in a bizarre twist concerning evidence the judge directed the jury to return a 'not guilty' verdict.

However, returning to our journey of 1960, from Broadstone the final set of rails to journey over were those of the original 1847 route to Hamworthy Junction (singled between these points in 1932). Departing on this line, the 'new' direct line to Poole falls away on the left, while soon on the right the aforementioned 1962 clay pit siding site is passed. Shortly after this the line left the borough for around ¾ of a mile passing mainly across heathland, in quick succession two sidings, one each side of Lytchett level crossing, were passed. The line then re-entered the borough before running into Poole's sixth and final station at Hamworthy Junction, and a link up with the other end of the 1893 causeway route coming in on the left across Holes Bay. This station was completely rebuilt in 1892 when the Holes Bay causeway was built, it has two platforms linked by a subway, with main brick-built buildings on the up side. A signal box stands on the down platform, which was graced with waiting room, etc. under a short canopy. This was, and remains, an island platform, the outer face of which once served the branch to Lower Hamworthy. The main line goes off ahead and curves right, passing on the left in the 'vee' formed with the branch the site where (until 1954) the third locomotive sub-shed once stood.

The rails leave the town ½ a mile further on at Rockley bridge where the railway makes its third harbour crossing of Lytchett Bay. From the junction the line to Lower Hamworthy heads south, to be described in detail later, whilst adjacent to the station was another pottery siding.

The 'Devon Belle' Pullman stock forming a travel agents' special to Weymouth is hauled by Bulleid 'West Country' class Pacific No. 34008 *Padstow* and is seen between Broadstone and Hamworthy Junction in the early 1950s.   *John Sansom*

Lytchett level crossing at Upton was situated between Broadstone and Hamworthy on the outskirts of Poole. This scene *circa* 1900 depicts what was to become part of the A35 road running between Southampton and Dorchester crossing the Southampton to Dorchester Railway.   *B.L. Jackson Collection*

Hamworthy Junction looking east, viewed from the small engine shed yard. The line to Lower Hamworthy is on the right. The photograph can be dated between 1885 when the class '46' engine No. 133 was rebuilt from a 4-4-0T to a 4-4-2T and 1903 when it was renumbered 0133. One of the locomotives nicknamed 'Hamworthy Buses' No. 133 departs toward Wareham, past the up goods yard (*left*).   *B.L. Jackson Collection*

Hamworthy Junction station looking west *circa* 1935 with 'B4' class 0-4-0T No. 103 in the branch platform. From the angle of the sun it would appear to be around 6 pm suggesting No. 103 is about to leave for Poole and a trip down the quay tramway. *Lens of Sutton*

Photographed in January 1968, Hamworthy Junction signal box looks shabby as it bears the grime from the passing of countless steam-hauled trains. In May 2007 the box still stands and controls access to the Hamworthy Goods branch, although it is normally switched out at weekends. *Colin Caddy*

A 1950s view of the exterior of the 1893 Hamworthy Junction station with the station master's house on the left.   *Alan Greatbatch Collection*

A second view east on 16th March, 1963 shows the station in more detail. On the left is the cattle dock, with island platform centre. BR Standard class '4' 2-6-0 No. 76012 is standing at the Hamworthy branch platform face.   *Colin Caddy*

Between 26th October and 2nd November, 1947 the track layout at the east end of Hamworthy Junction was extensively remodelled. The direct connection to the 'new' 1893 down line from the old Broadstone route was taken out and several other minor alterations made. This view of those works in progress was taken from the up starting signal. Down trains used the branch face of the island platform during this period (via the line next to the wagons).

Alan Greatbatch Collection

The east end of Hamworthy Junction 10 years later on 16th August, 1957 as class 'B4' 0-4-0T No. 30093 runs into the bay platform from Poole. Down trains from Broadstone now had to pass along the outer face of the island platform to regain the down main line at the western end of the station. *Wessex Collection*

Main Line Services

Passenger services in the summer at this time still saw Saturday holiday extras running both from London and the North of England, increasing the weekday total of 90 trains (45 down, 45 up) to 111 (57 down, 54 up). Add to this empty coaching stock movements and banking engines for Parkstone bank returning light for the next job, Poole could become pretty hectic on a Saturday.

After that, Sunday's total of 33 trains (15 down and 18 up) must have come as blessed relief to the signalmen in Poole's three boxes, especially those controlling the two level crossings who had the job of winding the gates open and shut. Trains passing through would take one of four routes:

Waterloo/Southampton to Swanage/Dorchester/Weymouth
Bournemouth to Templecombe/Bath/Bristol and the North via the S&D
Bournemouth/Poole to Brockenhurst (via Wimborne)
Bournemouth to Salisbury (via Wimborne).

Most Weymouth-Waterloo trains *c.* 1960 were normally worked by Bulleid Pacifics either 'Merchant Navy', 'West Country' or 'Battle of Britain' classes, or sometimes by a Nine Elms Standard class '5' '73XXX' 4-6-2. The Weymouth stopping trains saw 'U' class 2-6-0s, 'N15' 4-6-0s, 'H15' 4-6-0s, 'Lord Nelson' 4-6-0s, Standard class '4' '75XXX' 4-6-0s, Standard class '4' '76XXX' 2-6-0s, 'West Country' or 'Battle of Britain' Pacifics, 'Q' and on occasions 'Schools' class 4-4-0s and 'Q1' class 0-6-0s.

Salisbury services utilised the diminishing 4-4-0 'T9' class plus 'U', 'N' and Standard class '4' '76XXX' 2-6-0s. For a time in 1959 four displaced eastern section 'E1' class 4-4-0 Nos. 31019, 31067, 31497 and 31507 were allocated to Salisbury and worked down, but their use was short-lived. Brockenhurst 'Old road' trains used push-pull fitted 'M7' class 0-4-4Ts on the route until final withdrawal of the type in 1964 saw Ivatt class '2' and Standard class '3' '82XXX' 2-6-2Ts work out the line's final days. Engines off the S&D were '2P' 4-4-0, Ivatt class '2' 2-6-2T, Standard class '4' '76XXX', Standard class '4' '75XXX', Standard class '5' '73XXX', Stanier 'Black 5' 4-6-0s, '3F' and '4F' class 0-6-0s, '9F' class 2-10-0 and '7F' class 2-8-0, while other Southern freights produced mainly 'S15' class 4-6-0s, 'Q', 'Q1', '700' class 0-6-0s and the 'B4' 0-4-0T.

On occasions other locomotives appeared including Western Region (WR) engines, while three rundown Stanier class '3' 2-6-2T Nos. 40098, 40126 and 40171 worked in off the S&D in 1960.

For a rural non-industrial area a reasonable amount of freight was generated in Dorset, some of it coming through the Port of Poole, but by 1960 traffic levels began to decline. 'As required' freights did not run, daily pick-ups at local yards began to find less wagons to deliver/collect as the sending of railborne goods began to fall off. Most through freight trains called at Poole yard, whilst local trip freights started or terminated in the yard. Working times were as shown in *Appendix Three*.

Finally Poole yard on summer Saturdays was also the base for a couple of engines turned out specifically by Bournemouth shed for banking a procession of lengthy trains up Parkstone Bank, some of these being the usual services specially strengthened for the holiday season.

This then was what was visible to a rail traveller passing over the main line. But over the 150-plus years since the railway arrived in Poole there has been much more railway mileage of various gauges hidden within the borough and surrounding area. A large amount of these lines served industries involved with exploiting the underlying clay or Poole Harbour and its shipping, in some instances as will be seen, both.

Of the Poole routes described above, only the section from the Bournemouth boundary to Hamworthy, plus four stations at Branksome, Parkstone, Poole and Hamworthy remain within the borough. These lines and stations are served by electric-multiple-units introduced since 1988 to replace a diesel-worked service which had operated since the end of steam in 1967. Electrification of the line between Branksome and Weymouth saw, for a time, a frequency of three trains per hour running between Poole and London, but latterly this has been reduced to two per hour. The fastest service to London is 2 hour 5 minutes, hardly any quicker than in steam days! But it is now possible to be in London at 7.26 am, an hour before the first up steam service had even departed Poole for the capital at 8.25 am ('The Royal Wessex') which gave a 10.50 arrival in Waterloo. Since the withdrawal of the former inter-Regional trains from Poole and Weymouth (cross-country services now start/terminate at Bournemouth), just 98 weekday services pass through Poole and there is no perceivable difference denoting a winter or summer/holiday timetable.

Class '442' 'Wessex Electric' arriving at Poole on a Weymouth-Waterloo service on 2nd January, 2007. Sadly these superbly smooth riding and comfortable electric multiple units were withdrawn from South West Trains service one month later. This unit was a hybrid, comprising coaches from units 2413 and 2418.   *Author*

Main line passenger services through Poole in 2007 are entirely worked by German-built electric multiple units. In this view, taken on 7th February, 2003, one of the first such units to be delivered No. 450010 is seen sandwiched between match wagons *en route* to Branksome depot for commissioning. *Author*

For many years numerous inter-Regional trains either started/terminated or ran through Poole. Sadly 17th May, 2003 witnessed the last such train, A Virgin 'Voyager' No. 221131 *Michael Palin* runs out of the carriage sidings to form the 08.27 Poole-Aberdeen service. Departure of this train left both the town and the (old) county of Dorset devoid of cross-country services. *Author*

Freight in Dorset is at a low ebb compared with the past. Passing the former goods yard reception sidings empty liquid petroleum gas (LPG) wagons are being worked from Avonmouth to Furzebrook by class '60' No. 60025 *Joseph Lister* on 4th September, 1992. The LPG trains ceased running in 2005 and visits by class '60s' are now few and far between. *Author*

Freight services passing through Poole have been decimated, especially since the demise in 2005 of the twice-daily Furzebrook to Avonmouth Liquid Petroleum Gas (LPG) train. At present irregular trains of stone to Hamworthy are the only freight services actually serving the town, while a twice-weekly (Mondays and Wedenesdays only) sand train from Wool with corresponding empties (Tuesday and Thursday only) passes through. All sidings and private connections have long since been closed and removed; however, the former reception roads to Poole goods yard remain in use as an electric multiple unit turn round and servicing point. A massive reduction in Poole goods yard sees just three sidings remaining, however, further changes are due to take place. Plans announced in 2005 envisage the 1988 station buildings being demolished and new facilities incorporated within a massive redevelopment of the goods yard site. Luckily the sidings will be retained for engineers' use and to stable 'crippled' rolling stock, but in a realigned position more parallel with the main line. At Hamworthy Junction the branch to Lower Hamworthy still diverges, and here one railway item of note remains in Poole. The branch is protected by a fixed semaphore signal, reputed to be the last semaphore on the Waterloo to Weymouth route.

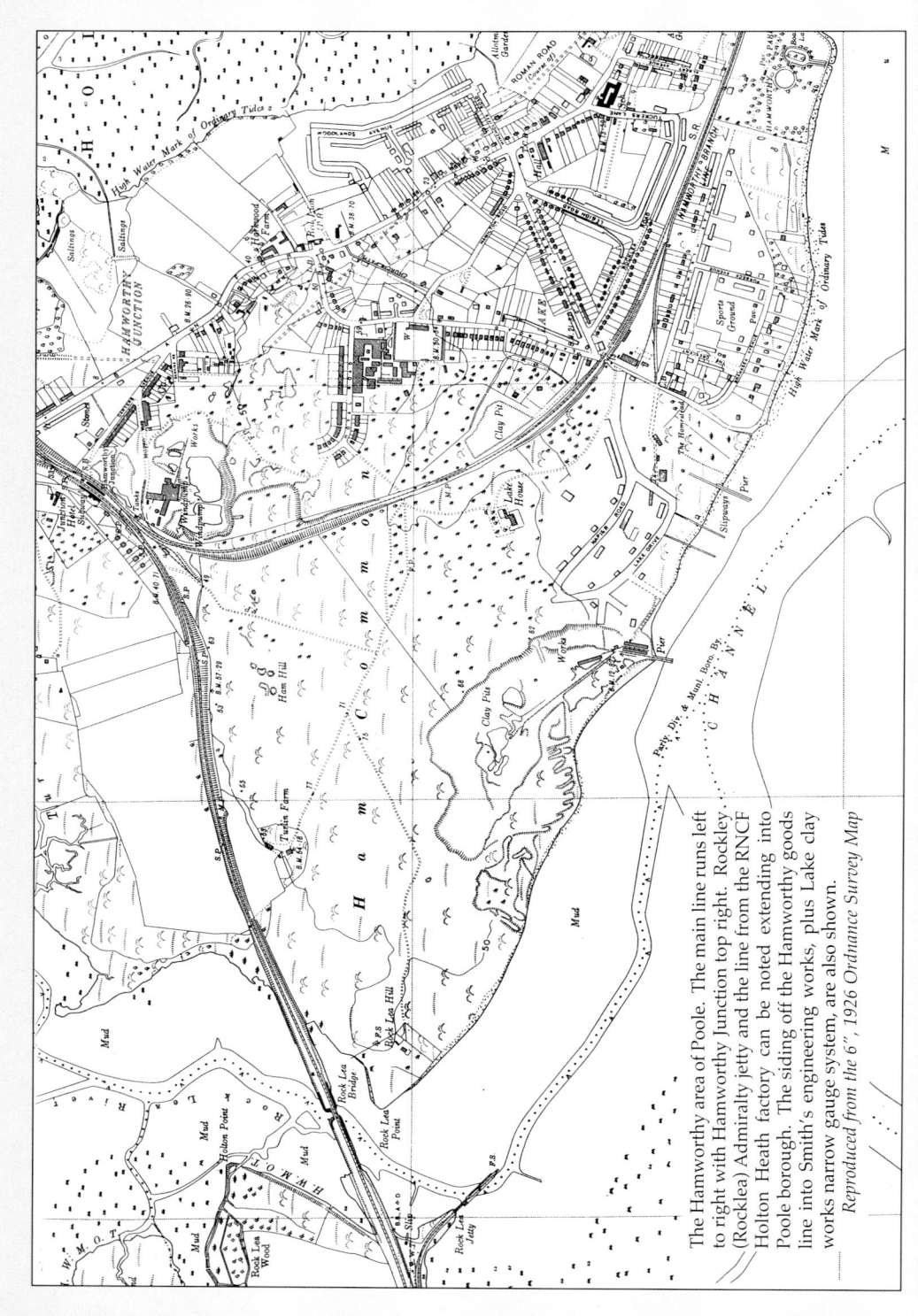

The Hamworthy area of Poole. The main line runs left to right with Hamworthy Junction top right. Rockley (Rocklea) Admiralty jetty and the line from the RNCF Holton Heath factory can be noted extending into Poole borough. The siding off the Hamworthy goods line into Smith's engineering works, plus Lake clay works narrow gauge system, are also shown.

Reproduced from the 6", 1926 Ordnance Survey Map

Chapter Two

The Hamworthy Branch, 1847 to 1967

For this history of the railway lines to the harbour and the Port of Poole, and given the fact that the first line into Poole is still in use, we begin with a study of this line. Its continued existence is most probably known to the legion of railway enthusiasts who specialise in photographing freight trains. It is almost certainly known by some local persons outside the railway fraternity by virtue of it running alongside Hamworthy Park.

The Hamworthy Goods branch, to give it its present day title, leaves the main London to Weymouth line at Hamworthy station to swing south and then pass between the Dawkins Road Industrial estate and the Royal Marine base. From here it descends at a gentle rate to cross Lake Road on (for road traffic) a low headroom bridge, the line continues parallel to Lulworth Avenue before crossing on the level Ashmore Avenue. The track then passes alongside Hamworthy Park at the rear of Hamworthy Middle school. Originally from near this point, the line ran along the shore line for the rest of its course. Later infilling of the harbour for the construction of Hamworthy Park, and then in the 1930s and 1970s for port extensions, has put it some distance from the water's edge and thus has released the railway company from the problem of erosion by the sea. At just under two miles from Hamworthy Junction the original Poole station is reached; access was via Station Road, now the entrance to James Bros Ltd, a steel supply and construction firm.

The Hamworthy branch was the first section of standard gauge railway constructed in Dorset; after its passage through Parliament the Southampton and Dorchester Railway Act received the Royal Assent on 21st July, 1845. The Act authorized a capital of £500,000 in £50 shares, being limited to £10 per share at intervals of not less than three months. The company was empowered to raise another £166,000 in mortgages and bonds once half the share capital had been subscribed, £380,000 being already paid up when the Act was obtained. Samuel Morton Peto, whose company, Messrs Grissell and Peto, had been awarded the construction contract, agreed to take shares worth £25,000, as part payment of the £420,000 he had quoted for building the line, Peto also advanced £800 from his private funds to enable work to start without delay. He had already taken the far-sighted step of shipping some materials into Poole whilst the Act was progressing through Parliament, it being the intention to build the Poole (Hamworthy) branch first then work out in each direction along the main line as land and resources became available.

By the end of August 1845 more than a mile of embankment had been raised across Hamworthy Common, but work further inland was deliberately delayed until after the gathering of the harvest to avoid the payment of excessive compensation. In April 1846 it was reported that the line was progressing well in the direction of Wareham despite some difficulties in obtaining solid foundations at Rockley, where the route crossed an inlet of Poole Harbour, and it was necessary to resort to pile driving, but to the east of Poole Junction little had been done.

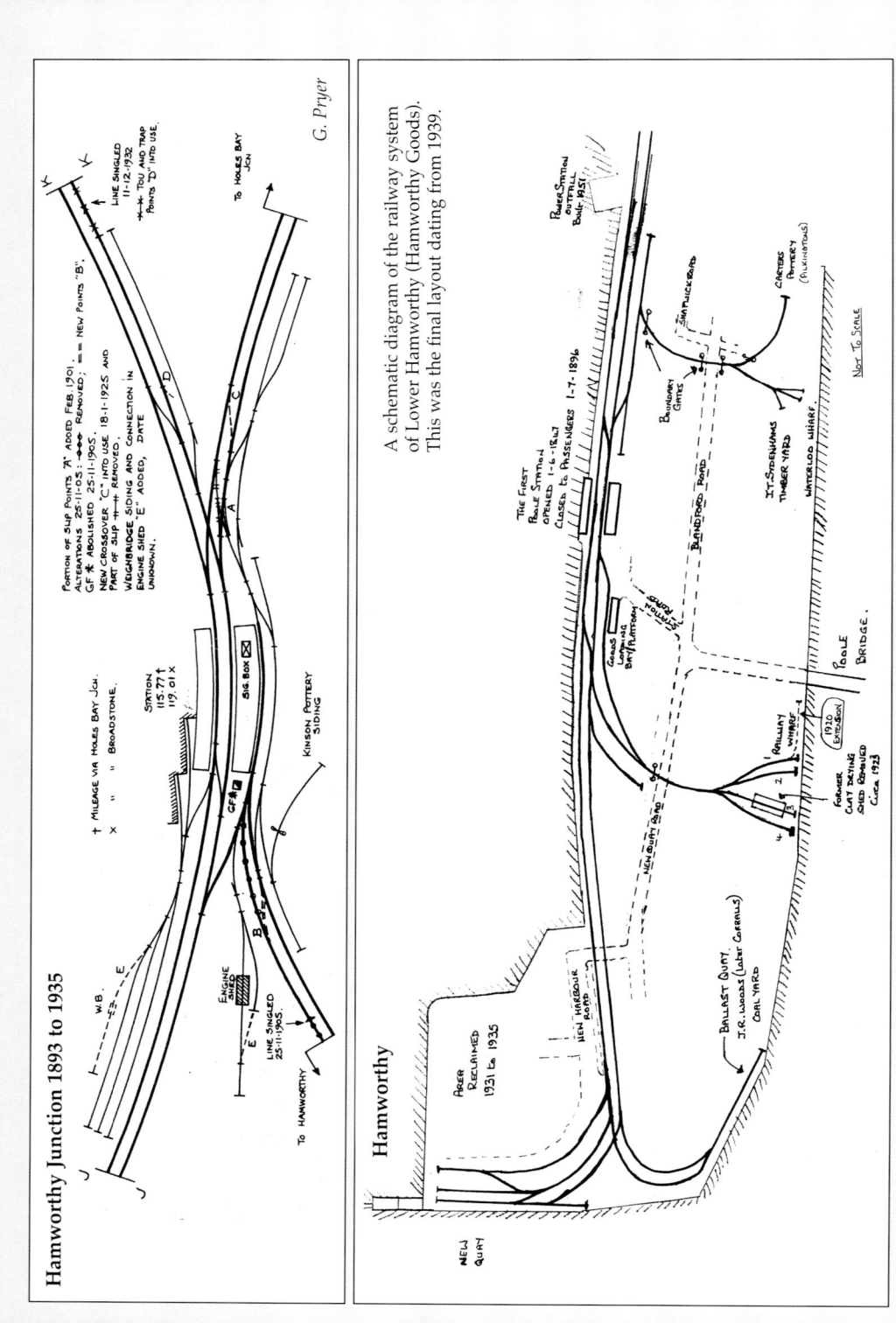

Hamworthy Junction 1893 to 1935

G. Pryer

LINE SINGLED
11·12·1932

---×--- TRAP AND TRAP
POINTS "D" INTO USE.

TO HOLES BAY
BAY.

PORTION OF SLIP POINTS "A" ADDED FEB 1901.
ALTERATIONS 25·11·05; --◆-- REMOVED; == NEW POINTS "B".
G.F.※ ABOLISHED 25·11·1905. ◆ ※ REMOVED.
NEW CROSSOVER "C" INTO USE 18·1·1925 AND
PART OF SLIP --※-- REMOVED.
WEIGHBRIDGE, SIDING AND CONNECTION IN
ENGINE SHED "E" ADDED, DATE
UNKNOWN.

STATION
115·77 †
119·01 ×

SIG. BOX ⊠

KINSON POTTERY
SIDING

† MILEAGE VIA HOLES BAY JCN.
× " " BROADSTONE.

W.B.

GF☒

ENGINE
SHED

LINE SINGLED
25·11·1905.

TO HAMWORTHY

Hamworthy

A schematic diagram of the railway system
of Lower Hamworthy (Hamworthy Goods).
This was the final layout dating from 1939.

RIVER STATION
OUTFALL
BORE 1851

CARTERS
POTTERY
(PILKINGTONS)

SHIPLUCKS YARD

BRIDGEWAY
GATES

J.T. SYDENHAMS
TIMBER YARD

WATERLOO WHARF

NOT TO SCALE

BLANDFORD ROAD

STATION
ROAD

THE FIRST
POOLE STATION
OPENED 1·6·1847.
CLOSED TO PASSENGERS 1·7·1896

GOODS
LOADING
BAY/PLATFORM

POOLE
BRIDGE.

1920
EXTENSION

FORMER
CLAY DRYING
SHED REMOVED
CIRCA 1923

2
3
4

RAILWAY
WHARF

NEW QUAY ROAD

AREA
RECLAIMED
1931 to 1935

NEW HARBOUR ROAD

BALLAST QUAY
J.R. WOODS (LATER CARRALLS)
COAL YARD

NEW
QUAY

Later that month the *Poole Herald* commented that the work was at a standstill due to bad weather. Once the weather improved work was resumed with vigour - although again most of the activity was at the western end of the line.

The Hamworthy branch was opened as single track but had been doubled by 1863, later due to the advent of the 'new' Poole station opening in 1872 passenger traffic began to dwindle. So much so that in 1896 the passenger service on the branch line was withdrawn. In 1905 the line reverted to single track as one set of rails (the old up line) was taken out of use and lifted. However, in 1916 during World War I, part of this 'up' line was re-laid as a long Admiralty siding back towards Hamworthy Junction across Ashmore Avenue crossing, to diverge into a site that later became J.R. Smith's engineering works yard. It then left the works yard to cross Lake Road on the level, near what is now the 'Yachtsman' public house. Here it entered (as it was then known) 'Auxiliary Shipyard Extension No. 62' then being built by the Government/Admiralty; the shipyard began production of some 1,000 ton concrete barges in 1917. Internally the shipyard sidings were almost certainly shunted from 1918 by a Kerr, Stuart 0-4-0ST (Works No. 3123) built and delivered in that year to the Admiralty.

Workers for this yard used a special train service to and from a platform known as Lake Halt constructed at the same period on the embankment by the low bridge over Lake Road. At the end of hostilities the Halt was closed and later demolished. After World War I parts of this shipyard were sold as surplus to military requirements and became the Gardiner Shipbuilding Co. and Smith's Ironworks respectively. The relaid railway line from the old station into C.J. later J.R. Smith's remained Government-owned until 1949 when British Railways assumed control to the yard boundary. It then saw use for deliveries to Smith's well into the late 1960s. However, the extension into the shipyard, being the responsibility of the Admiralty, was at an unknown date *circa* 1925 taken out of use and lifted, thus becoming one of the shortest-lived pieces of railway to give commercial access to Poole harbour waters. In World War II some of the yard again went over to war use as RAF Hamworthy flying boat base. Today part of the site off Lake Drive is retained by the Royal Marines, but most of it is beneath a prestigious housing development called Moriconium Quay.

It was, however, at the lower, terminus end of the line that the various rail connected wharves saw the most activity. The first of these handled one of Poole's heaviest imports, timber from the Baltic. Waterloo Wharf, or Sydenham's Wharf as it is more commonly known, was accessible from a siding adjacent to the railway station. Leaving railway premises through a gate in the boundary fence the line entered what was at the turn of the century a timber yard, later it became part of the premises of Carter's Pottery Ltd (off Shapwick Road and demolished 1994). Leaving this site the line made a level crossing (ungated) of the main A350 Blandford Road (rails were removed *circa* 1975). The tracks then entered the timber yard of J.T. Sydenham Ltd, where at the time of writing (August 2006) rails are still *in situ* between their sawmills and outbuildings. From here, a point leads one set of rails into another section of Carter's Pottery, now Pilkington's tile factory, whilst the track to the wharf

This view from the brakevan of a branch freight approaching Lake taken on 14th July, 1960 shows part of Doultons Clay pit on the left. This site, served by a siding from 1929 until 1964 (out of shot), is now a housing estate. The train engine is BR Standard class '4' 2-6-0 No. 76015

H.C. Casserley

This 1919 picture is the only known photograph of the short-lived Lake Halt on the Hamworthy goods branch. Built in 1916 twenty years after regular passenger services on the line ceased, it was served by a special train service conveying workers for a nearby wartime Admiralty shipyard. Brownsea Island is visible in the background. *Transport & Travel Monthly*

A view looking up the line toward Hamworthy Junction shows on the left the long siding re-laid from Hamworthy Goods in 1916 on the site of the old up line. The foreground connection to the branch was added in 1940, the siding served a World War I Admiralty shipyard. The partially visible section of the building was latterly used by J.R. Smith's engineering works.   *B.L. Jackson Collection*

An early engraving purporting to be the Pottery at Hamworthy. A certain artistic licence is apparent inasmuch as road and railway (Hamworthy Branch) have been transposed and St Michaels Church is portrayed somewhat nearer and higher than in real life.

B.L. Jackson Collection

'B4' class 0-4-0T No. 30093 arrives from Hamworthy Junction with the 2.00 pm branch freight on 30th April, 1957. To the right of the locomotive are the buildings of Carter's Pottery (demolished 1994), access to this site and J.T. Sydenham's timber yard was from the adjacent siding.
Hugh Davies (Photos from the Fifties)

The station at Lower Hamworthy was Poole's first station from 1847 until 1872 and the opening of the present station. This *circa* 1900 view shows the original Southampton & Dorchester Railway station buildings. The former up platform is just visible on the left.   *Lens of Sutton*

proceeds straight ahead into the timber yard. Here the line split into two sidings, one of which then splits again into two short stub sidings at an angle of 90 degrees to the wharf ending just short of the water's edge. Later they were roofed over and an overhead gantry crane spanned the tracks and adjacent hard standing. This wharf is visible on the Holes Bay side of Poole Bridge and is still occasionally used by a large vessel for unloading timber. The rails of these sidings would appear to have last seen the passage of railway wagons around the early 1960s when a road tractor was providing the motive power beyond the railway boundary. A couple of steel-sided, 16 ton, 4-wheeled mineral wagons possibly with coal or coke for the pottery were noted by the author being propelled across Blandford Road at around this time.

Next along the line were Railway Wharf sidings, later to become J.R. Wood Ltd oil wharf, it was closed as such by the successors to Wood in 2004 and is now in use as a production site for Sunseeker luxury motor yachts. This was called Railway Wharf as it was owned by the LSWR. Again these sidings were at 90 degrees or end on to the quayside. Rail access was made via an extended siding in the station goods yard which passed through a gate in the railway boundary fence, it then crossed New Quay Road on the level out onto the wharf. Long since without rails, the station goods yard and gateway existed until the site was sold and turned into a car park for employees of a local boat builders in 1998. For reference, the yard's location was adjacent to the access road into the car ferry terminal. Once across the road the single access line fanned out into four separate sidings; prior to World War I the main use of some of this wharf area appears to have been for the transhipment of ball clay from the Purbeck area, this clay having arrived across the harbour by barges.

Some went into railway wagons for movement to London, etc. whilst the majority of clay in the early years went onto large sailing vessels. It was then taken to Runcorn near Liverpool, to be transhipped back to barges once again for onward movement via canals to the potteries in the Stoke-on-Trent area.

On the map on page 68 the wharf sidings are tabulated as Nos. 1 to 4. No. 3 siding was spanned by a tall shed in the shape of an upside down 'V' where some of the clay was dried. When sail gave way to steamships No. 4 siding was generally used to berth the wagons holding the fuel or bunker coal for the steamers.

As mentioned the LSWR owned the wharf, it also owned Southampton Docks, and when during World War I that port became very congested it was to Poole that the railway company diverted the Jersey potato and tomato traffic for discharge at Railway Wharf. This traffic continued after the war until at least 1919. Two ships seem to have been in use chartered by the LSWR, each load per ship averaged around 200 tons, not in bulk as are today's cargoes, but in 'packages' usually barrels. It took between 40 and 50 dockers about six hours to unload this tonnage; the record for 1919 appears to have been on 14th June when 3,309 'packages' totalling 164 tons 5 cwt were unloaded in 3 hours 55 minutes.

The ships arrived at about 6 am, at first the cargo went directly into railway wagons located in sidings Nos. 1 and 2, (about ten, 4-wheeled, covered box vans in each). When these trucks were full the remainder of the cargo (which at times included apples, pears and grapes), went onto the quayside until a

In this view taken around 1935, some 40 years after passenger services on the line ceased, the original buildings remain in good condition but the canopies and shelters have been removed. Just visible on the left behind the old up platform are the waters of Poole Harbour. A 'B4' class 0-4-0T is seen approaching from Hamworthy Junction. *Stations UK*

BR Standard class '4' 2-6-0 No. 76015 waits to depart from Hamworthy Goods station on 14th July, 1960. This photograph aptly shows the close proximity of Poole's first station to the Harbour waters. Note the former up platform constructed out on to the shore line.

H.C. Casserley

This view looking toward Hamworthy Goods station reveals the crane of Messrs James Brothers Ltd, which they used to unload structural steel girders from bolster wagons in the adjacent siding.   *B.L. Jackson Collection*

A quiet scene at Hamworthy Goods on 27th August, 1954. This view up the line reveals a newly completed office addition to the 1847 station building. Behind the two railwaymen, on the wall of the 'lean to' shelter is the water supply pipe used to service the branch shunting locomotive. Also evident on the old up platform is a World War II gun position 'Pill Box'.

R.C. Riley/Transport Treasury

The Hamworthy branch, having been freight-only since 1896, is quite regularly visited by enthusiasts' specials conveying those wishing to ride over 'rare' track. This train, worked by class 'M7' 0-4-4T No. 30107, chartered by the Railway Enthusiast Club (REC) of Farnborough, visited the line on 7th June, 1958.   *Norman Simmons (Photos from the Fifties)*

This view of the same REC train reveals push-pull set 738 at the old station, the tour participants in what was a far more enlightened age are allowed to wander freely to photograph the area. The tender of what appears to be a 'Q' class 0-6-0 on the Saturday branch freight is evident on the old up line.   *R.M. Casserley*

The goods shed at Lower Hamworthy seen after years of disuse *circa* 1960.   *R. Gosling*

Hamworthy Goods yard viewed in 1953, the centre siding extended across New Harbour Road onto Railway Wharf.   *R. Gosling*

A *circa* 1960 view of Hamworthy Goods looking towards New Quay with a class '04' diesel in
view.   *S. Drew*

After the closure of the Poole Quay Tramway and the transfer away from the area of the 'B4'
dock tanks their duties were taken over by BR 204 hp 0-6-0 Drewry diesel shunting engines. This
included the Hamworthy Goods branch; in this view taken on 14th September, 1966, No. D2028
is seen crossing New Harbour Road from Hamworthy Goods yard (*right*) into Woods Oil
terminal, the former Railway Wharf.   *Paul Strong*

From 1931 to 1935 an area of Poole Harbour adjacent to Ballast Wharf was reclaimed from the sea and a 'New Quay' constructed. In 1936 work is underway laying rails for both the railway and travelling cranes. Note the contractor's Sentinel steam shunter at the seaward end of the layout and Brownsea Island prominent in the background. *Andrew Hawkes Collection*

A view of the same location taken in 2003. A truckline ferry leaves for Cherbourg passing a ship tied up at New Quay, a title that still holds some 60 years later! *Author*

Once shunted by 'B4' 0-4-0 tanks and the Hamworthy Wharf & Coal Co. shunters, New Quay, Hamworthy was by the 1960s the haunt of 204 hp diesel shunters. On 14th September, 1966 No. D2028 was caught in action. Also indicative of the change in rail fortunes the three road lorries in view were part of a fleet of vehicles conveying grain from Salisbury to Poole for export, in earlier times the railway would have been the carriers. Prominent in view is one of the 1936-installed mobile cranes.

Paul Strong

new set of empty trucks could be shunted into place. The shunting here was by the railway company's own steam locomotive. Loaded with empty barrels and baskets the ships left for return to Jersey about mid-afternoon, thus both out and home trips were partly made in darkness, assisting efforts to evade German submarines.

Poole acted as a major naval port during World War I and many thousands of tons of coal for the Royal Navy ships came down the branch during the conflict. After World War I Railway Wharf continued handling general cargoes whilst still in the ownership of the railway, but the clay traffic previously mentioned now went to the Stoke potteries by train directly from sidings on the Swanage branch line.

The area saw some alteration in the 1920s, the large clay drying shed was removed around 1924. A small area of the harbour waters, once part of a shipbuilding yard adjacent to Poole lifting bridge, was at some period infilled and the wharf extended up to the bridge. In 1926 siding No. 1 was angled round and lengthened to run along the new part of the wharf edge to end near Poole bridge. In 1927 a small 4-wheeled petrol-driven locomotive was bought new from Muir Hill by users of the wharf to shunt independently of the main line company (within the wharf area) and was given the name *Edith*. Later the wharf area and locomotive came under the auspices of Stephenson, Clarke Ltd.

Back on the 'main' line beyond the original goods yard one single line continued along the harbour shoreline before splitting into two sidings. These sidings again were end-on to the area known as Bulwark Quay and Ham Quay which they served, but both sidings were connected via a wagon turntable to a short siding laid along part of the wharf and parallel to its edge. The railway company's resident steam locomotive was used to place or remove wagons into these sidings, in all probability one held the empties whilst the other received the loaded examples. Motive power on and off the wagon turntable, thence along the quayside track, was most likely muscle power from half a dozen or so dock workers, or if available a horse. On one occasion whatever the motive power, its proved to be bit over zealous as a wagon rolled straight over the turntable and ended up in the sea. Adjacent to this wharf was Ballast Quay, which as its name suggests, had since around 1750 been used to load ballast into empty ships. However, by 1900 this practice had ceased, eventually by 1910 Ballast Quay had become a coal handling point leased to the Hamworthy Wharf & Coal Co. Ltd. To service this facility the LSWR carried out some alterations to the track layout in the area and by 1920 had added a new connection from one of the two sidings. This connection was laid on a sharp curve which led into a headshunt from which a trailing siding ran along Ballast Quay. The 'Wharf &' part of the title was soon dropped, possibly when taken over by Harris Jenk Ltd who operated as the Hamworthy Coal Co. Cargoes of coal came in aboard the archetypical 'dirty British coaster with a salt-caked smokestack' bringing household coal from Yorkshire via Goole and Scottish coal from Methil.

In 1926 the Ballast Quay coal operation was taken over by Southern Roadways Ltd, this company set about expanding and improving the operation. Within a year steps had been taken to modernise the site, new plant including a brand new coal transporter was erected in 1927. Next in an effort to

Above: This 1953 photograph depicts the access line from Hamworthy goods yard to Railway Wharf passing through J.R. Wood & Co.'s oil storage terminal. Construction of this facility in 1950 saw the end of steam locomotives passing on to the wharf. BR engines only returned when the class '03'/'04' diesel shunters were introduced to the area in 1960. *Author's Collection*

Right: Hamworthy, New Quay is the setting for this 1954 photograph which depicts cider apples being discharged from a ship's hold into a waiting railway wagon partially visible centre left. *Author's Collection*

free themselves from having to rely on the Southern Railway (successors to the LSWR) moving wagons to/from the coal yard, Southern Roadways set about purchasing a shunting locomotive. In 1929 they bought from local firm J. Smith Ltd an ex-Portland Dockyard 0-4-0ST locomotive built in 1896 as Works No. 1496 by Bagnall of Stafford, the locomotive soon acquired the name *Iris*. J. Smith Ltd traded as James Smith, Ironworks, Lake Road, Hamworthy and are referred to on an earlier page, the rail connection into their works is illustrated on page 71. J. Smith dealt in the buying and selling of industrial equipment including steam locomotives, until at least 1937, when they were recorded as selling an engine to the British Sugar Corporation. This company ceased trading in 1994, by then they were trading as J.R. Smith (J.R.S. Southern) a structural steel stock holder and engineering supplies company.

In 1931 the track layout was altered yet again, the wagon turntable at the end of the two SR main line sidings being moved to a position at the dead end of the 1920 Ballast Quay siding. A second connection off the turntable was laid to connect to one of the SR sidings a few yards below the 1920 connection. Later in 1935 Southern Roadways purchased a second locomotive, a 1918-built Hawthorn, Leslie 0-4-0ST, Works No. 3360. This engine had seen use at the RNCF, Holton Heath factory, it came to Hamworthy in two or three pieces (boiler and cab etc.) and had to be re-assembled on site. The locomotive was re-assembled by coal yard staff led by Lionel Kerley, a gentleman who was to feature in the end of steam workings at Ballast Quay. The locomotive received a hand-painted name, *Little Audrey*, applied to the saddle tank above cast No. 16 number plates which it retained from its RNCF days. Purchase of the second engine could well have been prompted by the heavy traffic using the coal facility.

A picture of Hawthorn, Leslie 0-4-0ST (Works No. 3360/18) taken at the Ballast Quay, Hamworthy in 1935 soon after the locomotive had been purchased for use in the coal yard. The engine had arrived from its former workplace the RNCF, Holton Heath in pieces and had been reassembled by coal yard staff. It was christened *Little Audrey* by them but retained its former RNCF cast No. 16 number plates. Both of the coal yard's other locomotives *Iris* and *Edith* are just visible in the background   *Bob Clark Collection*

Above: Waterloo or Sydenham's wharf was served by three sidings. In this *circa* 1920 view all three are visible, the two right-hand tracks terminated close to the wharf edge. The yard rat-catching dog and at least 56 of Sydenham's timber yard staff are visible, some of whom are standing on loaded railway wagons.
Andrew Hawkes Collection

Above: A ship discharging some of the 1919 Channel Island potato and fruit crop is seen at Hamworthy, Railway Wharf. In view are two box vans and barrels of potatoes waiting to be loaded.
Left: A view of the same ship alongside Railway Wharf. Behind the vessel and soon to be demolished is the old clay drying shed.
(Both) Railway & Travel Monthly

The 1930s were particularly hectic, at times one ship was unloading with two more standing off awaiting a berth. In those far off days in such busy times the yard worked around the clock and staff were allowed to work 'back to back' shifts. It was not uncommon for workers to work a full day, take a one or two hour break, usually in the 'Shipwrights Arms', and then return to work through the night. Once several of the staff worked for several days and nights without going home, a practice which would not be allowed by today's Health & Safety Executive even if today's 'workforce' were willing to undertake such a task! Six loaded wagons at a time were taken to the two SR sidings, some had to be 'fly shunted' into the parallel siding. For those unfamiliar with this practice a wire hawser was attached between the locomotive and wagons, the locomotive them moved off down one siding and took up the slack in the hawser, points were quickly changed to allow the wagon to traverse the adjacent line. Once again the Health & Safety Executive would frown on this potentially dangerous practice, but it worked, and at Hamworthy without any serious consequences. A large proportion of this coal was *en route* to the RNCF Holton Heath factory where *Little Audrey* had once worked. Also in World War II the company was extremely busy supplying coal to the various Army and Navy bases and RAF airfields set up around the area. Ownership of the engines changed in 1936 when Stephenson, Clarke and Associated Companies Ltd took over the coal business from Southern Roadways.

Major outgoings from these two wharves which arrived by rail in the early to mid-1920s were tiles plus large consignments of scrap iron coming from companies breaking up surplus World War I equipment, whilst large amounts of timber were shipped in for onward rail movement.

One other part in Poole's seaborne communications was way back in 1848, and later in 1865, when the line carried passengers for two abortive attempts at inaugurating cross-channel passenger ferry services. Prohibited from owning or running its own shipping services, the LSWR formed a separate concern solely for this purpose known as the New South Western Steam Navigation Co. Initially running a service from Southampton, this company soon opened offices at the lower end of Poole High Street. Pre-empting Truckline Ferries (latterly Brittany Ferries) by 122 years, on 2nd May, 1848 the company's paddle steamer *Dispatch* left Poole on her maiden voyage for the Channel Islands and France. This service then operated throughout the summer of 1848 using the vessel *South Western* and was advertised in the newspaper *The Poole and Dorset Herald* thus:

London to the Channel Islands via Poole in the time of 11 hours. Our unrivalled steamships will leave Poole Harbour with goods and passengers for Jersey and Guernsey every Tuesday and Friday at three o' clock am after arrival of the mail train. Returning from Jersey every Wednesday and Saturday mornings at eight o'clock.

After arrival in Jersey with the Friday service the ship sailed on to St Malo or Granville in France. Fares ranged from 34 shillings first class London-Jersey to 14 shillings Poole-Jersey for a second class forward cabin. The LSWR had plans to expand the service and applied to build wharves, warehouses and landing places at Hamworthy, but the service was short-lived. This was due to objections from the Admiralty with regard to the effect new wharves would have on navigation, also some local ship owners objected, as did Poole council.

It should be stated that the Poole Council objection stemmed from 'sour grapes' with the LSWR over the siting and building of the station at Hamworthy. The council supposition was that the station should have been in the old town of Poole reached via a bridge across the Holes Bay outlet channel. Losing patience with the situation the LSWR decided to quit Poole for shipping services, the final sailing from Poole on 30th September, 1848 being an ignominious affair as the ship went aground. Passengers had to be taken off to continue their journey on another vessel as the '*South Western* awaited the next high tide to be re-floated'. The next attempt at a ferry service came 17 years later, by the late lamented Somerset & Dorset Railway* which connected with the LSWR at Wimborne (later in 1885 at Broadstone via a new line through Corfe Mullen) and had running powers into Lower Hamworthy/Poole.

In 1865 the S&D instigated a Poole to Cherbourg ferry service as the third leg of an ambitious Cardiff to Paris service. The plan entailed passengers leaving Cardiff on the ferry service operated by the S&D for a 1½ hour crossing of the Bristol Channel to Burnham-on-Sea. From there they would take an S&D train running via Glastonbury, Wincanton and Blandford to Poole, transferring here once again to a boat for a 6 hour crossing to Cherbourg. Finally another train on the Western Railway of France got the weary traveller into Paris somewhere near midnight! The service ran for only two summers using the paddle steamer *Albion* chartered from a Liverpool-based company. In the June of 1866 she left Poole at 12.30 pm on Mondays and Thursdays, the connecting train the 8.05 am from Burnham having arrived in Poole at 12.05 pm. Unfortunately the service was never profitable, so in August 1866, after three return trips from Cherbourg saw the ships complement of 'passengers' stand at 179 sheep and 85 pigs, the service was discontinued! Another 120 years were to pass before a successful passenger-carrying cross-channel ferry service began operating from Poole, and ironically from Hamworthy in sight of the old railway station. However, between 1926 and 1936 there was a sporadic 'passenger' service over the Hamworthy branch. The word passenger is in inverted commas because it was indeed a single passenger in the form of the eccentric Lady Houston. Thrice married Lady Lucy Houston DBE, was born in 1857 as Fanny Lucy Radmill. Later she became a chorus girl known as 'Poppy', her first husband leaving her £6,000 per annum for life. However, her main fortune of £5.5 million came after the death in 1926 of her third husband, shipping magnate Sir Robert Houston. With the money came a luxury yacht the *Liberty*. As a tax exile Lady Houston lived in Jersey travelling to the mainland on the *Liberty* sometimes via Poole. On such trips to and from Jersey Lady Houston would charter her own personal railway coach which would as necessary be attached/detached from a main line train at Bournemouth or Hamworthy Junction to be worked along the branch to gain access to the yacht.

Although not relevant to local railway history it may be of interest to note that Lady Houston gave £100,000 to the Supermarine aircraft company so that they could enter the 1931 air race for the Schneider Trophy. Success in that race led to the development of the Rolls-Royce 'Merlin' aero engine. In 1933 she also

* In 1875 the Somerset & Dorset Railway was taken over jointly by the Midland Railway and the London & South Western Railway to become the Somerset & Dorset Joint Railway.

provided the money for the Houston-Mount Everest flight expedition in which aircraft flew over Mount Everest for the first time and attempted to drop the British flag on the summit. She died in 1936.

The old LSWR along with the other railways in Southern England had been amalgamated in 1923 into the Southern Railway (SR). In 1931 changes were afoot as infilling of the harbour now began for the construction of a new quay complete with a new road called New Harbour Road to provide access. This work was completed in 1935; 72 years later the wharf still operates under the title of 'New Quay'. A short time after this the railway company began a series of changes to the track layout to suit the new circumstances. Firstly the line from the old goods yard to the New Quay was doubled. Next these tracks were, from new point work and via some quite sharp curves, angled round south onto the 'new quay', and north onto the old Ballast Quay and Hamworthy coal company's yard; these alterations were completed for use in June 1939 just before the start of World War II.

During the war years from 1939 to 1945 the branch, as in World War I, saw very heavy use bringing in fuel for the Navy boats and both the civil British Overseas Airways Corporation (BOAC) and RAF flying boats which used Poole Harbour. Shipbuilding materials for Bolsons' shipyard, who were building mine-sweepers for the Navy, plus other items vital to the war effort were also carried. All the British railways were pressed to the limit and beyond moving war materials as well as the usual everyday items such as food stuffs and coal, etc. Coastal shipping was suspended as the ships would have made good targets for German U-boats. Most materials were moved by rail and this included wagon loads of British grown timber for J.T. Sydenham in lieu of wood from the Baltic. Until replaced by a road tractor in the late 1940s, horses were used to pull the wagons to and from the main line. Now-retired employees of Sydenham's remembered this practice from the years of the World War II. When, *circa* 1985, some of these old hands were asked about the rail workings, the following tale came to light.

Apparently one of the horse handlers of those war days was a nasty ill-tempered fellow, being particularly brutal to the poor beast so employed. On one occasion needing to draw two trucks away from Sydenham's yard, the handler went between the wagons to couple one to the other. The old type of three-link chain wagon couplings were heavy and made a distinct clanging sound during coupling and uncoupling, which of course the horse knew well. On this occasion, on hearing the sound, the horse moved forward and the chap was partially crushed between the trucks. His injuries were sufficient to prevent his return to work; nobody, it was stated, was sorry to see him go, those old timber workers also maintained that the horse got his revenge by moving off purposely.

The New Quay area was guarded by the military and as part of local defences in case of German invasion a gun position 'Pill box' was built on what was once the up platform of the old station. All civilian workers entering the area were challenged by the sentries on duty. One night in the blackout in a scene reminiscent of the popular TV series 'Dad's Army' a rookie sentry issued the familiar challenge, 'Halt who goes there!' The approaching Ballast Wharf coal yard worker expecting one of the regular sentries replied impatiently, 'Me, who

Ballast Quay, Hamworthy on 16th February, 1933. Bagnall 0-4-0ST, Works No 1496 built in 1896 and named *Iris*, was photographed shunting coal wagons for Stephenson, Clarke Ltd, later J.R. Wood/Corralls, the former Hamworthy Wharf and Coal Co. The engine originally worked until 1929 at Portland Naval Dockyard. *Mark Yarwood/Great Western Trust Collection*

Another view of the 1896-built Bagnall *Iris* the ex-Portland dockyard shunter. She is seen on Ballast Quay with Poole Town Quay just visible in the background. *Bob Clark Collection*

the bloody hell do you think it is, a Jerry', to which the nervous rookie replied, 'Advance Me and be recognised! When later in the war the south coast areas including Poole became restricted zones, the railways again showed their worth by moving vast amounts of men and materials for the 1944 D-Day invasion.

After World War II the years of exhaustive war effort by Britain's railways had left the national system in a rundown condition; however, changes were on the horizon. With the Nationalisation of the railways on 1st January, 1948, British Railways was born.

Part of this process saw the former Southern Railway relinquish its ports and docks interests such as Southampton; in Poole this meant Railway Wharf. Parallel to these events the 1940s had seen a new company J.R. Wood Co. Ltd appear on the scene to take over the Hamworthy Coal Company from Stephenson, Clarke & Associated Co., whilst the wharfage interest of Stephenson, Clarke transferred to Southern Wharves Ltd.

Southern Wharves had been involved with the management of Railway Wharf but now took control of its marketing, part of the area being developed by J.R. Wood as an oil terminal opening as such in 1950. The fact that highly flammable liquids were on site in Wood's oil storage terminal saw the demise of British Railways (BR) steam engines running onto Railway Wharf. From that time Wood's coal handling operations, in the main, were concentrated on Ballast Quay, the exception being pre-bagged coal and boiler fuel such as coalite, anthracite and ovals. This was supplied to the local coal merchants from an area of the old Railway Wharf adjacent to Poole lifting bridge and served by the extended siding No. 1, any wagons for the coal facility being moved by *Edith*.

The majority of general cargoes on the Hamworthy side of Poole's quays were now being loaded or unloaded at New Quay as the new mobile cranes and railway lines running parallel to the quay edge made the process easier. One consequence of this was that Southern Wharves ordered from the Darlington company of Robert Stephenson & Hawthorn Ltd two 0-4-0 saddle tank locomotives. These locomotives, Works Nos. 7544 and 7545, were built and delivered in 1949 and became No. 1 *Bonnie Prince Charlie* and No. 2 *Western Pride*, replacing the elderly pair of maidens *Iris* and *Little Audrey*, both of which were cut up on site in 1950 by Bakers Ltd, a Southampton-based scrap merchant.

When put to work on Ballast Quay and New Quay the locomotives saw use turn and turn about, one in service, one on standby. The standby engine was kept inside a purpose-built engine shed where minor repairs and maintenance was also undertaken; it befell the duty engine to remain outside in the elements. When the weather was particularly inclement the home-made doors fitted to the right-hand side of the locomotives, the side of the prevailing south-west winds, were shut tight (see photograph of *Bonnie Prince Charlie* overleaf). Driven by Southern Wharves/J.R. Wood coal yard staff, they moved wagons to and from British Railways, on to the quays for loading and unloading under the coal grabs and cranes. No evidence has come to light that they ever ventured up to Railway Wharf via BR tracks through the old station goods yard, their sphere of operation being solely limited to the section of line below the level crossing of New Quay/New Harbour Road.

In 1949 Southern Wharves Ltd as successors to Stephenson, Clarke decided to replace the two locomotives working at Ballast Quay. Two Robert Stephenson & Hawthorn 0-4-0 saddle tanks were ordered, the first, Works No. 7544 *Bonnie Prince Charlie*, is seen in the coal yard on 16th August, 1957. *Wessex Collection*

In 1964 *Bonnie Prince Charlie* had a 'bit part' in the film *Heroes of Telemark*, partly shot in Poole. In the film as actors Kirk Douglas and Richard Harris confer on the deck of a ship 'Charlie' is to be seen shunting on New Quay in the guise of a Norwegian engine under control of his regular driver Mr Kerley. During filming a wooden nameplate bearing the name 'Oslo Havnevesen' was stuck over 'Charlie's' own nameplate, even though the engine was too far into the background for the nameplate to be read. Incidentally this ship also had railway connections, in the film, which portrays an actual heroic World War II event, the ship bore the name *Galtesund*. In actual fact she was the *Roebuck*, a freighter built in 1925 for the GWR who set her to work on Weymouth to Channel Islands cargo traffic. For the filming contract she was brought to Poole from Weymouth and had her funnel painted white. In the film after the *Galtesund/Roebuck* sails from 'Oslo', i.e. New Quay, she is hi-jacked, and crosses the North Sea to 'Scotland'. This was Poole Town Quay adjacent to the former terminal point of the Poole Quay Tramway just a mere 600 yards across Poole Harbour! Such is the illusion created by the cinema industry. *Roebuck* last sailed from Weymouth in railway service on 27th February, 1965 and was scrapped in July 1965.

Corralls Ltd took over J.R. Wood in 1960, later on the dissolution of Southern Wharves in October 1962 they also assumed responsibility for their two engines. This was no surprise as over the years Wood's staff had driven and maintained the engines. The engines remained in regular use until Corralls decided to replace them. On 6th September, 1965 *Bonnie Prince Charlie* was transferred to work on Dibles Wharf, Southampton, travelling there overnight under its own steam.

False wooden nameplate carried by *Bonnie Prince Charlie* during filming *Heroes of Telemark*.

Driven by Mr Kerley, who was accompanied by a British Railways driver, 'Charlie' left Hamworthy cab leading at around 6.30 pm and travelled up the branch to Hamworthy Junction and on through Poole to conquer the 1 in 60 of Parkstone bank. Arrival at Bournemouth just on dusk was to a blast of whistles from the assembled main line engines as she entered the BR engine shed to be turned to face chimney first for Southampton. After midnight 'Charlie' pottered off up the main line with a stop for water and a bearing check at Brockenhurst before continuing through the New Forest to its new home. 'Charlie' remained in service at Southampton long enough to be bought and preserved, and can be seen at the Didcot Railway Centre, Oxfordshire.

Western Pride was not so lucky; she remained in use until March 1966 when a replacement 54 horse power Hibberd 'Planet' four-wheeled diesel, Works No. 2054, built 1938 was purchased from Poole Gasworks. *Western Pride* was then cut up for scrap by a Southampton-based company. On closure of Poole Gasworks a second four-wheeled diesel was purchased, this was an 88 horse power Ruston, Works No. 242867, dating from 1946. It was towed from the gasworks to Hamworthy Goods by a BR diesel on 22nd February, 1973. Discovery of this information indicates that the 'Planet' was most probably towed to Hamworthy as well. From that date the Hibberd became a standby engine until the cessation of regular seaborne coal to Ballast Quay in 1976; it was then purchased for preservation. On Saturday 26th June, 1976 it was transported to the Swanage Railway, becoming the first locomotive to arrive at their fledgling operation. Given the name *Beryl*, it still remains on their stocklist. For the next nine years the Ruston was the only industrial standard gauge locomotive at work in Poole shunting loads of incoming railborne coal. Eventually in July 1985 transport of coal by rail over the Hamworthy branch came to an end and the Ruston was left to gather rust on the quay side.

By 1986 Corralls had become a subsidiary of PD Fuels Ltd and this company decided not to renew the lease on the Ballast Quay site. A proposal to sell the Ruston to Western Fuels for use at Wapping Wharf coal concentration depot, Bristol did not materialise. As the Ballast Quay site was now being cleared for use by Poole Harbour Commissioners the future of the engine looked bleak. Michael Day, a local railway enthusiast, informed the Swanage Railway that the locomotive was up for sale for a price of £1,000. Unwilling to acquire the engine, the Swanage group offered the information that the Bodmin & Wenford Railway (B&WR) was looking for its first working locomotive. Mr Day informed PD Fuels of the merits of the B&WR scheme and they agreed to donate the engine to the railway provided the B&WR supplied the transport to move it. Thus the shunter was handed over on 24th May, 1986 and moved to Bodmin, but the present status of the engine is not known.

For 12 to 15 years from the Nationalisation of the railways until the mid-1960s all sorts of traffic were handled on the branch, imports transferring to rail included such things as cider apples, grain, timber, etc. and for a short while after World War II the Jersey potato traffic once again came to Poole. But coal was the heaviest traffic, mostly being moved from J.R. Wood's Ballast Quay yard. The 1960 freight timetable shows that goods trains left at 12.20 pm and 3.45 pm and a third as required at 4.50 pm. Railborne goods onto the line for export still arrived but began to decline as lorries began to make their mark, General merchandise was still buoyant and handled in reasonable quantities in the station goods yard for local companies.

Right: The all important BR 'footplate pass' issued to Mr Kerley for *Bonnie Prince Charlie*'s epic jaunt from Poole to Southampton.

Below: A view of 0-4-0ST *Bonnie Prince Charlie* taken inside Bournemouth engine shed on the evening of 6th September, 1965. The gentleman leaning against the locomotive is Lionel Kerley, the regular driver of 'Charlie' at Hamworthy. Mr Kerley had brought the locomotive over to Bournemouth from Hamworthy and was about to set off to Dibles Wharf, Southampton with the engine. He was accompanied and supervised by BR driver Percy Green and fireman Richard Steel.

(Both) Bob Clark Collection

BRITISH RAILWAYS BOARD Nº 9580
British Railways SOUTHERN Region -3 SEP 1965
FOOTPLATE & DRIVING COMPARTMENT PASS
The Bearer MR. L. KERLEY
Non, B.R.B. Personnel is authorised to Ride
Upon   In the driving compartment of
Main Line } Locomotives   Diesel } Trains
Shunting   Electric
                    (Rear cab only)
......19/35.... train from .Bournemouth.. to Southampton
Between ....HAMWORTHY...............
and ....SOUTHAMPTON.... P. B. TAYLOR
until / on .....-6 SEP 1965. DIVISIONAL MANAGER
              (Delete as necessary)
Issued for the B.R.B. by....................
This pass to be shown when required and is issued subject to
the conditions printed on the other side.   B.R. 87102
              OPERATING OFFICER

The other RS&H locomotive delivered new to Ballast Quay in 1949 is seen at Hamworthy in 1954. Note the wire hawser on the front buffer beam used for the odd bit of fly shunting.
Ivo Peters courtesy of Julian Peters

Another view of *Western Pride* at Ballast Quay showing the locomotive coaled up ready for the following day's work. *Ivo Peters courtesy Julian Peters*

Ruston-Hornsby 88 hp 4-wheeled diesel Works No. 242867 built 1946 is awaiting its fate in early 1986 at Ballast Quay, Hamworthy. Coal operations on the wharf had recently ceased rendering the locomotive redundant, it later went to the Bodmin & Wenford Railway in Cornwall. *Michael Day*

Steel arrived for James Bros steel erectors, and on occasions also went to J.R. Smith's Lake Road works; this steel came from the northern or Welsh steel works. The Cement Marketing Co., later Associated Portland Cement Marketing (APCM), had a depot on New Quay and received bagged cement by rail. These bags were unloaded direct to its premises from covered railway vans as they stood on the curve from New Harbour Road round onto New Quay. This practice continued until APCM moved its operations to a new depot at Hamworthy Junction. The former cement depot was used to store steel coil for a while before being demolished in 2006.

Goods trains arrived at 7.49, 11.40 am and 2.09 pm and a fourth as required at 6.15 am. This high level of activity was due to the fact that the railway was still by law the 'Common Carrier'. For those unfamiliar with this term, the railway was obliged by an Act of Parliament going back to the early days of railways, to carry at a designated rate of charge (in relation to size) any feasible package or load, large or small as requested by any person or concern. This ruling saw such things as a circus or even complete farms being moved, i.e. livestock, farm machinery, even unused hay and the farmer's belongings going on a special train. At the other end of the scale you could arrive at your local station with a parcel no larger than a box of matches and send it by train. However a certain Dr Richard Beeching was about to change all this! He was appointed in 1961 by the Government of the day as Chairman of British Railways to re-structure the railways and reduce the £100 million loss the railway had incurred. The fact that one of the Government ministers involved with this appointment, one Ernest Marples, had major connections with the roads' lobby and the construction of the M1 motorway has over the years prompted massive controversy! Beeching's infamous report *The Re-shaping of British Railways*, published in 1963, was to have far-reaching consequences for the carriage of goods on the railway. It also left a legacy of lost railway mileage: the full folly of this action has only now been realised.

July 1967 saw the end of trains hauled by steam locomotives on the line as steam was withdrawn on the Southern Region of British Railways. From that date diesels would haul the one or two booked trains per day.

Chapter Three

The Hamworthy Branch since 1967

Total dieselisation began in July 1967, and in the years since steam's demise the line has seen mixed fortunes as traffic levels have fluctuated wildly. The Beeching report was acted upon and vast mileages of BR were closed. The Hamworthy branch escaped this fate but the station goods yard saw drastic reduction of of use with the rescinding of the 'Common Carrier' Act and resultant rise in freight charges. Coal was still shipped in at Corralls (J.R. Wood) Ballast Quay for transfer to railway wagons until 1976 and the cessation of seaborne coal into the Port of Poole.

One curiosity concerning coal from Ballast Quay which lasted until the early 1970s is perhaps a contender for the shortest run on BR of wagon load freight. Local Hamworthy area coal merchants Hooper Brothers were (and still are) based close to Hamworthy Junction; coal for them was off loaded from ship into rail wagons for transport in the branch freight to the Junction station. Here the wagons for Hooper's were tripped over to the up side sidings where they were off-loaded after only two miles of rail haulage.

In an earlier chapter mention has been made of Wood's/Corralls' boiler fuel operation on Railway Wharf, some of this coal came in by rail and, after the demise of the wharf-based 4-wheeled petrol engine *Edith* in 1966, BR locomotives once again ventured onto Railway Wharf. Wagon loads for this coal facility were moved onto the wharf by BR 204 hp diesel shunters, where internal movement was by a rubber-tyred road tractor which either towed them with a wire hawser or propelled them via a sleeper lashed to its front end. This machine was given an unofficial nickname of 'Muriel'; on occasions 'Muriel' also operated across New Quay Road onto BR property at the goods yard in lieu of a BR locomotive. After the end of shipborne coal to Ballast Quay the local domestic coal handling and distribution facility was transferred to this area of Railway Wharf. This saw the major coal flow reversed as it now came down the branch in steel-sided 16 ton mineral wagons to supply this facility until March 1986 when both Railway Wharf and Ballast Quay coal yards finally closed.

The mid-1970s reclamation of more of the harbour for a roll-on, roll-off ferry terminal promised much but delivered little. On 16th June, 1976 an overbridge clearance run was undertaken by class '33' locomotive No. 33021 leading a short rake of container flat wagons. The leading flat was loaded with one container, this test run saw particular attention given to Poole High street footbridge. With the level crossing gates closed to road traffic, No. 33021 drew to a stand across the crossing, pedestrians then watched incredulously as various persons descended from the rear cab of the diesel complete with an extension ladder. Erecting the ladder one chap then ascended and proceeded to measure the gap above the container! With the job done, the ladder was ceremoniously lowered and reloaded on to the locomotive, everyone reboarded the engine and off they went to Hamworthy Goods! This set the stage for a two month trial container service in early 1977 (10th January to 7th March). At this time 70 containers per

A scene at Hamworthy Goods in 1976, a train load of cars for export aboard the MV *Clearway* has been split, the half on the old up line is being made ready for unloading whilst the second portion is being reversed into position for similar treatment.   *Fred Worth*

Class '33' No. 33019 is seen on 18th April, 1979 at the 'top end' of the Hamworthy branch with a lightly-loaded Freightliner from Hamworthy Goods bound for Millbrook Freightliner terminal. The sidings of the APCM terminal are visible left.   *Anthony E. Trood*

week were being dispatched by road from the Port of Poole, estimates made at the time assumed that by 1980 at least 500 containers per week would be dispatched on 3 trains per day. With the trials over, a planning application for a permanent site was made and had been granted by May 1978.

Next a 'Section B' Government grant was applied for, to cover some of the estimated cost of £400,000 of installing the container loading facility. To handle the containers once off the ships, a loading gantry spanning both tracks leading to New Quay was erected by the Freightliner sector of BR, whilst an adjacent tarmacadam hard standing area was also laid. All work was completed by early 1979 and on Monday 23rd April, 1979 the first regular Freightliner service ran from Hamworthy. Once a day (Monday to Friday) the service began running as an extension of the Freightliner railway operation to and from Southampton, Millbrook, generally hauled by a 1,550 hp class '33' locomotive. Booked arrival time at Hamworthy Goods was at 3.00 pm with departure at 5.25 pm. The service, using a short rake of Freightliner flat wagons, began well with the train loading to full capacity at the outset. But load levels declined and failed to reach anything like the 1977 estimate of 500 containers per week. Soon the train was running with perhaps just one container, sometimes it even ran empty. Not unnaturally BR Freightliner withdrew the service and it ceased running in January 1981.

At around the same time large quantities of cars for import and export on the ship MV *Clearway* passed through the port, Rover cars and vans going out and French cars coming in. Most were transported on long trains of 25 double-decked car transporter wagons, each wagon conveying 8 to 10 cars (200 to 250 vehicles per train). Being heavy trains they were hauled by a more powerful 2,580 hp class '47' locomotive. On arrival the train was split in half, each half was then shunted up to the New Quay Road level crossing and mobile ramps positioned end-on to the wagons. The cars were then driven off the train, down New Harbour Road and onto the ship, or vice versa. This traffic was lost when the ship diverted to a competing port.

Also tried for a short period in 1982 by a company called Novatrans was the transporting of an Intermodal type of container known as COMBI (Caisse Mobile) using the old Freightliner gantry. This service saw limited use and could not have been classed as a success, these trains regularly brought the unique 1,500 hp class '73' electro-diesel locomotives onto the line working on their auxiliary 600 hp diesel engines. Local traffic to the goods yard declined until only the odd single wagon load for a local company or a steel consignment into James Bros, steel stockholders, remained, the final load of steel for them (one wagon) appears to have been unloaded on 29th December, 1979.

When the class '08'/'09' came to the branch in 1977 the working pattern changed as these locomotives were confined to shunting at Lower Hamworthy with the occasional *sortie* from 1985 up to the new Hamworthy Junction cement terminal. The branch was now served by just one direct freight service from Eastleigh, the locomotive/s of this service on arrival at Lower Hamworthy worked various trips to either Branksome depot, Wool or Hamworthy Junction as required. The booked return was at 1.18 pm to Eastleigh.

The shunting yard remained open for general freight and merchandise until March 1981 when facilities where withdrawn and transferred to Poole goods

The short-lived Freightliner service from Hamworthy used a loading gantry erected in 1978, by 1981 the service had ceased. In this view taken on 3rd March, 1983 class '09' No. 09026 approaches the gantry as it takes wagons to New Quay to be loaded with steel coil.

Anthony E. Trood

Also in 1983 No. 09026 passes under the gantry with steel billets loaded at New Quay.

Author

yard, although it still handled coal for Corralls' Railway Wharf facility. After cessation of coal traffic and the freight from Eastleigh in July 1985 the connection to Railway Wharf was severed on 31st August and a buffer stop was installed. Its function along with the rest of the former goods yard changed to wagon holding sidings for the only remaining cargo to transfer from 'ship to rail' to be carried out within the Port of Poole, imported steel from Belgium and Holland.

Three types of steel were carried, strip steel in large coils for the Rover car-making plant at Swindon initially went out in old wooden-bodied 4-wheeled wagons covered by a tarpaulin, these being replaced by larger wagons for a time. Eventually purpose-built covered wagons were used leased from Powell, Duffryn Ltd by John Carter, their name and logo being carried on the canvas cover of these wagons. Unfortunately the carriage of this type of steel went over to road haulage in 1993. Large slabs of steel were also carried at certain times, but not in great quantity or with any regular frequency. The third and probably the most consistent type of steel cargo to leave the Port of Poole by train were large heavy steel billets. During the years 1981 to 1990 the steel imports were steady and consistently heavy, reaching a peak in 1989 (94 train loads were noted) enough to warrant extra trains on some Saturdays.

A downturn in steel imports was evident in 1990 (57 train loads went out) this continued in 1991 as only 29 train loads were noted departing from Hamworthy. Not only were there less trains but some of those that did run were often lightly loaded. When in August 1991 No. 08760 failed during its 40 mile journey from Eastleigh and blocked the line near New Milton for several hours, the viability of the Hamworthy line was brought into focus. Thus, early in 1992, British Railways announced that the Hamworthy Goods branch was to close as and from 31st March that year. At that time the line employed on a five day week basis four or five railwaymen engaged in loading the wagons, plus a driver on the BR shunting locomotive. Running costs were high as they included those incurred when the class '08' or '09' shunting locomotive had to travel 40 miles to Eastleigh for major maintenance every six weeks or so. Originally these shunting engines were allocated to Branksome depot and outstationed a week at a time at Hamworthy Goods. But BR sectorisation in the 1980s had seen Branksome become a Network SouthEast (NSE) depot, thus the shunters were transferred to Eastleigh. From that time through the good offices of NSE the locomotives were stabled at Branksome at weekends when they were refuelled.

British Rail was at this time being prepared for privatisation and loss-making parts of the system were ripe for closure, the Hamworthy branch proving to be no exception. Nevertheless the closure announcement came as somewhat of a surprise locally. Luckily Poole Harbour Commissioners (PHC) considered the branch an asset to their then current operation, thus PHC were not about to allow it close out of hand. To their credit, PHC, and to an extent Poole-based shipping agents John Carter, brokered a deal with BR whereby the railway track below the new ferry terminal level crossing down on to New Quay became the responsibility of PHC. They were also to take over the loading of the rail wagons as well as providing a shunting engine, complete with driver. To this end BR continued to provide services throughout April 1992, however, in May

On 2nd October, 1984 two class '33s' Nos. 33010 and 33034 are seen dropping down from Hamworthy Junction to Holes Bay causeway. They have just regained the main line from the Hamworthy Goods branch. Their train consists of covered wagons containing coils of sheet steel bound for Swindon.   *Anthony E. Trood*

Before being sold the APCM terminal at Hamworthy was in use for its original purpose receiving cement powder for around 12 years from 1975 to 1987. In this view taken on 8th February, 1984 class '47' No. 47229, which had failed, is being rescued by sister engine No. 47131.   *Anthony E. Trood*

A view up the line at Hamworthy Goods on 16th May, 1989. In view is class '37' No. 37197 at the head of a steel train to Swindon and Cardiff. The BG behind the locomotive had received attention from the Carriage & Wagon Department and was being worked away in the consist.
Gordon Griffin

At the top end of the Hamworthy Goods line on 3rd February, 1999 sister locomotives Nos. 37803 and 37710 sit on the branch with a load of stone from the Mendips whilst the train is unloaded over the fence into the former APCM site. Later a purpose-built concrete pad was laid in the site to allow fragmentised scrap steel to be loaded. *Paul Kneller*

Hamworthy Goods on 16th June, 1989 and class '33' No 33202 with the weed killer train. The locomotive is seen at the level crossing between New Quay Road on the right and New Harbour Road (behind the photographer). It was at this spot car transporters were loaded/unloaded, mobile ramps were placed end-on to wagons shunted down both tracks to 33202's position. Cars were then driven direct on to the crossing tarmac and down the road onto the ship.

Author

The last Hamworthy shunting turn undertaken by BR on 8th May, 1992 was most appropriately carried out by class '09' No 09025. So long a Hamworthy resident she received an unofficial hand-painted allocation code HW. After being withdrawn from BR service the engine went into preservation at the East Kent Railway.

Author

With the cranes on Ballast Wharf at Hamworthy visible on the skyline two class '37' locomotives Nos. 37109 leading 37293 wait for departure time with a load of steel billets bound for Cardiff on 4th September, 1992.   *Author*

A Powell Duffryn type PXA wagon used to transport steel coil for the automotive industry is seen at Hamworthy Goods. Note the name of Poole-based shipping agents 'John Carter' applied to the wagon sheeting.   *Terry Saunders*

An' 8F' class 2-8-0 in Poole once again, the former Turkish State Railways No. 45160 is seen in the APCM terminal at Hamworthy in November 1990. This locomotive was built by the North British Locomotive Co. in 1940 and allocated LMS No. 8274. It was, however, sent to Turkey by the War Department as WD No. 348. Repatriated to the UK in 1989, the engine ran for a short time on the Swanage Railway until withdrawn from service for an overhaul. The overhaul was begun at the Hamworthy site, however restoration operations were transferred to the Gloucester & Warwickshire Railway when the APCM site was acquired by new owners.   *Author*

The Port of Poole on 7th July, 1992 saw three redundant ex-BR class '20' locomotives awaiting export to France for use on the Chemin De Fer Departmentaux. The locomotives in question were formerly BR Nos. 20035, 20063 and 20228.   *Author*

1992 Allied Steel & Wire Co (ASW) of Cardiff, as recipients of some of the steel loaned PHC one of their shunting locomotives. This gesture helped overcome the initial lack of motive power and the engine remained at Poole until November 1992 whilst PHC located an engine of their own.

British Rail's costs reductions came by withdrawing its staff and shunting engine, locomotive No. 09025 performing the last shunting duty for BR on 8th May, 1992. BR also reduced the amount of main line trains to service the steel flow from five to two per week, to be worked on an 'as required' basis. This deal between PHC and BR saved the line, further economies came about when BR drafted in more powerful locomotives to work the steel trains. Around the time of these events the port saw an interesting railway export, but as the loads concerned were not passed to run over BR metals, their arrival unfortunately was on road transport low-loaders. Four ex-BR class '20' type '2' diesels had been purchased by the French railway company Chemin de fer Departmentaux (CFD Industries). After overhaul at Crewe works they went to their new home in central France via the Poole-Cherbourg roll-on, roll-off ferry service. Ex-BR No. 20139 slipped out in June 1992 unrecorded, but when locomotives Nos. 20035, 20063 and 20228 followed on 7th July, 1992 the movement was noted and photographed. New coach body shells for both London Underground and Irish Railways have been imported through Poole, but only for onward movement by road.

Imports through Poole of the steel billets which were consigned to ASW, Cardiff remained constant for well over 20 years. Amounts varied from just one loaded 'BDA' bogie bolster wagon to the 22 loaded 'BDAs' which went out on 2nd August, 1996. This train saw the weight of billets standing at around 815 tons, the total train weight in the region of 1,200 tons presenting a challenge to the locomotive at the head of the train, especially when climbing the 1 in 60 of Parkstone bank.

In 1997, five years on from the brush with closure, the branch was fast approaching 150 years of existence. As the week prior to the 150th anniversary date of 1st June arrived, so did a pleasant surprise in the form of a locomotive on a route learning trip from Westbury. The Wiltshire crews were familiarising themselves with the route from Eastleigh to Hamworthy Goods. This was in readiness for a new flow of traffic proposed for the branch, stone from quarries in the Mendip hills was to be transported to the old disused Associated Portland Cement depot close to Hamworthy Junction. From the cement depot, by now in the hands of Oasis Plant Ltd, onward delivery of the stone was to be by road the relatively short distance to a new by-pass road under construction around the Dorset villages of Puddletown and Tolpuddle. After five weeks of route learning the first load of stone arrived on 2nd July, 1997 behind one of the Quarry company's own American-built class '59' locomotives. These stone trains ran from that date almost every weekday, and on Saturdays as well between May and December 1998 by which time the by-pass had been completed.

From January 1999 the stone terminal has been acting as a local distribution point, but due to lower demand trains now run as required. Sidings complete with a run-round loop within the 1975-built cement terminal had unfortunately been removed for scrap less than a year before the stone trains started running.

The 1893-built causeway from Poole to Hamworthy Junction across Holes Bay in Poole Harbour sees class '60' No 60 092 *Reginald Munns* passing over it on 12th April, 1995 with steel billets bound for Cardiff. Calls for a road bridge 'fixed link' over this area has a hollow ring when viewed against this under-used and visually less intrusive asset.   *Author*

'Welcome to Poole' greets disembarking ferry passengers today. No doubt this was the sentiment echoed by the civic dignitaries on 1st June, 1847 when the railway arrived in the town. The closest date to the 150th anniversary that a train ran to Hamworthy Goods was 30th May, 1997. Class '60' No. 60 089 *Arcuil* is seen on that day beneath the sign as the driver receives instructions from EWS supervisor Paul Kneller.   *Author*

Therefore unloading is done by a mechanical grab 'over the fence' as the train stands on the branch line. When unloaded the empty trains run down to Hamworthy Goods for the locomotive to run-round the train before departing back to the Mendip Quarries. The year 1998 saw a new commodity come to the branch in the form of fragmentised scrap metal. Five Tiphook Rail wagons were included in the consist of the incoming empty steel train on 14th July, 1998. The wagons were part of a trial and, as with the stone trains, these wagons were loaded 'over the fence' from the Oasis Plant site. The scrap was transported to South Wales and the trial was deemed a success, therefore further trains were booked to run.

To ease loading of the trains Oasis Plant Ltd subsequently laid a large concrete pad to accept the scrap brought in from a local scrap merchant. The efforts of Oasis Plant to encourage more freight to rail and to the Hamworthy branch in particular is very laudable.

A Steady Decline

During 1999 the branch was quite busy, the levels of scrap being transported steadily increased until scrap wagons often outnumbered the loaded billet wagons. Steel billets were being imported through Poole on an annual contract basis but were lost to Newport docks at the contract renewal date in May. Throughout June and July scrap was the only steel transported over the line, but on 27th July a ship arrived conveying more billets. It transpired that Newport docks were unable to handle the billets in the manner ASW wished and thus Poole (and rail) regained the traffic. A further upturn in fortunes materialised on 8th November when a train load of steel coils arrived in SNCF (French Railway) wagons direct from a French steel making plant via the Channel Tunnel. The Port of Poole was now being used as a steel stock holding point, thus steel coil was stockpiled in various PHC buildings before onward movement within the UK.

These shipments via the Tunnel continued into 2000, the last being noted on 13th March, 2000. Billets for delivery to ASW Cardiff continued to come in via Poole and travel forward by rail. Unfortunately Newport docks revised their handling procedures and regained the import contract, the last load of billets leaving Hamworthy Goods on 5th May, 2000. Scrap steel, however, was still buoyant and continued through the year. A small ray of hope for more traffic came on 17th October when a trial load of large slab steel was sent out; alas it proved to be a one-off.

Scrap and stone trains kept the branch fortunes buoyant throughout 2001, but the scrap was nearly lost when Railtrack suggested the wagons were (inadvertently) being overloaded. The train of 6th July was stopped at Swindon and run over a weighbridge where some axle weights were found to be exceeded, the whole train weighing in at a massive 1,850 tons. This is believed to be the heaviest train to have been worked up the 1 in 50/60 Parkstone bank by a single locomotive (No. 60023), a testament to the hauling power of a class '60'. Oasis Plant then brought in loading apparatus equipped with a weighing

Class '60' No. 60063 *James Murray* is caught on camera *circa* 2000 at Hamworthy Goods having run round its train. It is awaiting departure with a consignment of fragmentised scrap steel for Allied Steel & Wire Co., Cardiff. This freight flow ceased when ASW went into receivership in 2002.   *Gordon Griffin*

In May 2005 several trains were once again loaded with scrap, this time destined for Newport, South Wales for export to China. As the usual contractors were unable to load the train, Poole Harbour Commissioners undertook the loading at New Quay with their mobile crane. The PHC locomotive is visible to the right of the crane.   *Author*

device, ensuring the continuance of the flow, in total 33 trainloads of scrap went out to ASW during the year. Unfortunately in July 2002 ASW went into liquidation, the last normal load of fragmentised scrap being dispatched to them on 5th July; however, the official receiver handling ASW affairs sanctioned one further consignment which departed on 19th July.

This was a major blow to the revenue accredited to the Hamworthy branch, the loss being marginally offset by a small of 'crumb' of traffic which had commenced on 11th April. The traffic in question was Contaminated Oil Waste (COW) which came from the extensive oil industry based in and around Poole and Purbeck. The COW was coming from the BP oil rig based on Furzey Island within Poole Harbour and was brought over to the mainland by barge in large square tanks. The tanks were loaded onto wooden-bodied 4-wheeled 'OBA' wagons and transported to Lowestoft for recycling/disposal. At the outset the flow was small with just four trains running in 2002 (two empties in, two loads out). More encouraging was the recommencement of steel coil trains in October, a trial trip from Poole to Wolverhampton steel terminal proving successful. After the trial a 12 month contract saw at least 21 loads of coil transported from the PHC stockpile to Wolverhampton during 2003, more good news came with the resumption in February 2003 of the fragmentised scrap metal. Once again the scrap was loaded at Oasis Plant site and was railed to Newport docks where it was exported to Spain/Portugal. Unfortunately, neither contract was renewed, bulk movement of coil reverting to road haulage from December 2003.

Poole Harbour Commissioners locomotive is seen arriving at Hamworthy, New Quay on 11th April, 2002 with the first set of OBA wagons loaded with empty tanks. The tanks will be transported by barge to Furzey Island to collect Contaminated Oil Waste from the oil pumping station.   *Author*

During the year someone worked out that transporting scrap by rail from one port to another, while good for the rail industry, was a bit of a pointless exercise! Therefore once again the scrap traffic was lost from the Hamworthy branch in December 2003 when the scrap was loaded onto ships at New Quay Poole for direct delivery to Spain/Portugal.

The year 2004 witnessed very low levels of traffic on the branch with just eight COW movements and four movements of steel coil over and above any stone trains. The same trend was followed in 2005 with 17 COW trains, although three fragmentised scrap trains ran in May. In this instance far off China influenced Poole rail traffic, that country's insatiable need for scrap forced prices up; it was once more railed to Newport docks to be loaded onto large ships for transport to the Far East. By now Oasis Plant were unable to handle scrap so PHC carried out the work at New Quay giving employment to the PHC shunting locomotive. Once scrap prices slipped back to lower levels the Spanish/Portugese direct shipping service became viable again and is still operating. A final blow came in February 2006 when the transport of the COW went over to road transport leaving just the 'as required' stone trains as the only rail traffic to traverse the Hamworthy branch.

Seen arriving at Hamworthy Goods on 3rd January, 2003 is EWS class '66' No. 66088 with a rake of wooden-bodied OBA 4-wheeled wagons loaded with empty tanks. The square tanks will be transhipped into barges and taken to Furzey Island to collect Contaminated Oil Waste. The tarmac area between tracks is where the Freightliner containers were once loaded.
Author

Chapter Four

Motive Power on the
Hamworthy Branch

Although the official opening date of the Southampton to Dorchester line and the branch to Poole (Lower Hamworthy) is quoted as 1st June, 1847, the very informative book *A History of Poole* by C.N. Cullingford gives a date of 21st May, 1847 for the first train. This, however, was the Board of Trade inspector's train which travelled the full length of the line prior to operating permission being granted. The fact that on its return to Southampton the train was derailed seems not to have caused any major problems or delay to the opening.

The earliest reference discovered is that a locomotive named *Reindeer* hauled the first train. As photography was in its early days not many early pictures of trains or locomotives exist from that period, with hardly any taken in the Poole area. The next reference found is to an 1852-built engine No. 34, a 2-2-2 well tank named *Crescent*, which was working the line in the early 1850s.

By the 1870s 2-4-0 No. 116 *Stromboli* was at work on the line, it was built in 1869 at the Nine Elms, London works of the LSWR to the design of locomotive superintendent Joseph Beattie. A day's work for the driver and fireman spanned nearly 16 hours, beginning at around 6.30 am. At 6.50 am the engine took empty coaches down to Poole, i.e. Lower Hamworthy, where it carried out shunting duties in between working six passenger, one mixed and two goods trains over the branch, all return trips (18 trips total), the day ending at about 9.30 pm.

All this was done six days a week, 52 weeks per year on locomotives with no cab, just a weatherboard for protection against wind, rain or cold, and that only when going forward. Holidays were one day at Easter and part of Christmas day. The branch engine was kept in an engine shed situated in the fork of the main line and branch line at Hamworthy Junction station. There was no Sunday service so the driver got the day off, but the fireman was expected to be at the shed to supervise the labourer employed to wash out the locomotive boiler and ensure the engine was cleaned and made ready for working on the following Monday. The working man's lot was certainly arduous in the 1800s. From 1893 until 1897 a Manning, Wardle 0-6-0T No. 459, formerly named *Sambo*, was engaged in shunting at the lower end of the Hamworthy branch.

By 1893 all of the main LSWR system to be constructed locally was in place and through trains were running from London to Weymouth via Southampton, Bournemouth and Poole. Therefore it was decided to withdraw the branch passenger service and as from 1st July, 1896 any main line locomotive going down the branch after this tended to be 0-6-0 goods engines, although other locomotives types would have put in appearances. This would have included some 'Metropolitan' 4-4-0 tank engines and their replacement Adams class '46s', converted in 1886 from 4-4-0T to 4-4-2T. From 1907 some of this type saw out their days working from Bournemouth shed, usually one or two were outbased at Hamworthy where they were used on local services. This included passenger trains on the main line causing them to win the nickname of 'Hamworthy Buses'. By 1899 the Hamworthy goods shunt was in the hands of another Manning, Wardle 0-6-0T No. 392, the former *Lady Portsmouth*.

Manning, Wardle-built LSWR 0-6-0T No. 459, formerly *Sambo*, one time Hamworthy Goods shunter, is seen at Nine Elms *c.* 1895.   *Norman Collection, courtesy of the South Western Circle*

Above: 'B4' class 0-4-0T No. 103 shunts at Hamworthy Junction on 10th August, 1934. Visible behind the engine is Kinson Pottery which had its own siding. Note the driver's head gear! *R.W. Kidner*

Right: Bonnie Prince Charlie is at Hamworthy Junction in 1949 aboard a well wagon being delivered brand new to Southern Wharves Ltd.
Terry Williams courtesy of Alan Greatbatch

However, 1899 was the year that Poole Quay tramway was cleared for steam locomotive operation, from then until 1960 that line and the Lower Hamworthy Goods yard shunt turn shared motive power in the form of 0-4-0 tank engines. It was decide to base these shunting engines at Hamworthy Junction engine shed which was now a sub-shed of the then new Bournemouth depot. For ease of use the shed trackwork was altered for an increased allocation which now included two 0-4-0Ts and two other tank engines. The other tank engines were at first the aforementioned 4-4-0Ts, followed in turn by the Adams 4-4-2Ts and then some 0-4-4Ts. These engines worked the local trip freights and shunted at Hamworthy Junction. The 0-4-0 tank engines, and the 'B4' class in particular became synonymous with the Poole Quay line and as such they are described in detail in a later chapter.

Locomotives assigned to the shed reached a peak of six in 1937 during Southern Railway days, but after World War II just one 'B4' class 0-4-0T and one 'M7' or 'T1' class 0-4-4T saw out their time until the shed closed on 3rd May, 1954. For the final years of steam the branch shunting engine travelled over from Bournemouth each day.

During the war Hamworthy had an early taste of the future in the shape of an 0-6-0 150 hp diesel-mechanical shunter. The locomotive was built by Hunslet of Leeds in 1934 for the London Midland & Scottish Railway (LMS) as its No. 7053. In October 1939 the locomotive was requisitioned by the War Department and gained the number WD23, by January 1941 WD23 was on loan to the Southern Railway. After working at Eastleigh locomotive works the locomotive spent some time in April and June 1941 on the Hamworthy branch and at Bournemouth locomotive depot.

The branch in British Railways days throughout the 1950s remained steam worked, types regularly noted being ex-LSWR '700' class 0-6-0 dating from 1897 and ex-SR 'Q' class 0-6-0 of 1938. The stark wartime Austerity SR 'Q1' class 0-6-0 of 1942 put in appearances, whilst the most common British Railways Standard locomotives to be seen were the class '4' 2-6-0 '76XXX' series introduced in 1953. The beginning of the end for steam on the branch came with the arrival of diesel shunters, by 1965 (on paper at least) the remaining freight trains were booked for diesel shunter haulage. However, until steam was withdrawn on the Southern Region of BR in July 1967, steam engines still appeared on some of the daily freights including the BR Standard class '4' 2-6-4 tanks. Latterly as steam traction was phased out and passenger train engines were demoted to freight work, once or twice in 1965 the branch saw the impressive 'West Country' and 'Battle of Britain' locomotives work down the line.

Apart from the ex-LMS shunting locomotive referred to earlier, diesel locomotives first appeared locally in 1959 when Drewry 0-6-0 204 hp shunting engines (later known as class '04') Nos. D2274 and D2275 came to the area. As their numbers increased so did their sphere of operation, ranging from Bournemouth station pilot duties to goods yard shunter at Poole. After closure of the Poole Quay tramway in 1960 they took over the remaining duties of the 'B4' class steam locomotives working between Poole, Hamworthy Junction and Hamworthy Goods. In 1964 No. D2180 was allocated to Bournemouth depot, the first of the similar BR-built engines (later classified '03') to come to the area. From then the two types worked turn and turn about without either taking particular preference on the Hamworthy line. The Drewry and BR 204 hp engines worked the Hamworthy branch, as the 'B4s' had done, shunting the yard, moving wagons to and from New Quay and tripping wagons to and from Hamworthy Junction. Their use eventually saw BR locomotives

An unidentified ex-Southern Railway wartime-built Bulleid designed 'Q1' class 0-6-0 heads for Hamworthy Goods and is about to pass Hamworthy Junction locomotive depot.   *OPC*

Hamworthy Junction locomotive depot dated from the opening of the Southampton & Dorchester Railway. Originally it housed the locomotive employed on Hamworthy branch services. It later became a sub-shed of Bournemouth finally closing on 3rd May, 1954; at its peak, in the 1930s, six locomotives were allocated to the depot.   *Author's Collection*

Class 'B4' 0-4-0T No. 30093 stands at Hamworthy Goods station on 16th August, 1957.

Wessex Collection

Maunsell 'Q' class No. 30539 is at Hamworthy Goods working the branch freight on Saturday 7th June, 1958. An REC special train headed by 'M7' class 0-4-4T No. 30107 is seen in the background.   *Brain Connell (Photos from the Fifties)*

Drewry 0-6-0 204 hp diesel shunter (later class '04') No D2275 stands at Hamworthy Goods on 14th July, 1960, two months after taking over the branch duties from the 'B4' class steam locomotives. Note that the engine is being re-fuelled from a road tanker, this was due to the lack of facilities at Bournemouth steam locomotive depot. Only when steam had finished and the new depot at Branksome had opened in 1967 were proper fuelling facilities available.

H.C. Casserley

The Drewry shunters were displaced by 275 hp 0-6-0 class '07' shunters ex-Southampton Docks in 1975. In this view No. 07010 prepares to leave Hamworthy Goods with a trip freight to Poole Yard. The locomotive is now preserved on the Avon Valley Railway. Note the old up platform has been eroded by wind and rain in the years since the photograph above was taken.

Jeff Anderson

work once again from Hamworthy Goods yard across New Quay Road onto Railway Wharf. As diesel locomotives they posed no greater fire hazard in the J.R. Wood oil terminal than the road tankers using the site. By 1965 lower traffic levels meant the 204 hp shunters were no longer spending all day on the branch, a revised diagram saw the branch served by two trip freights from Poole Goods yard. Both trips were booked for diesel shunting locomotive. The diagram began on Monday morning when the engine left Bournemouth depot at 6.15 am to run light engine to Poole, the booked workings Monday to Friday were then as follows:

Poole dep. 6.50 am, Hamworthy Junction from 7.02 until 7.35 (to detach wagons), Hamworthy Goods arrive 7.50. After shunting here until 9.00 the engine then ran light engine to Hamworthy Junction for shunting 9.10 to 10.15. A return to Hamworthy Goods at 10.25 saw an 11.15 departure with freight to Poole (arr 11.50). If required the locomotive worked light engine to Branksome goods yard. A booked return into Poole at 2.20 pm was in time for the 2.30 pm Poole to Hamworthy Goods trip working (arrive 2.59). The final trip freight departed Hamworthy Goods at 4.40 pm for a Poole yard arrival at 5.13 pm where the engine stabled overnight.

The locomotive returned to Bournemouth Depot on Friday evening or Saturday morning, dependent on whether the 6.50 am ex-Poole and 11.35 am ex-Hamworthy Saturday-only services were required. In the 204 hp diesel shunter years up until July 1967 and the end of steam on BR Southern Region, some or all parts of the diagram could, on occasions of high loadings or diesel failure, be covered by a steam locomotive. At the end of the steam era the diesel shunting locomotives were transferred to the new diesel/electric depot at Branksome.

The class 204 hp diesels worked until replaced by 275 hp '07' class 0-6-0 dock engines engines displaced from Southampton Docks in 1975. This was a case of history repeating itself for a third time as these '07s' followed in the footsteps of several ex-Southampton Dock Co. locomotives and the LSWR 'B4s' all of which had been ousted from Southampton to Poole. These '07' class engines, of which four, Nos. 07002, 07010, 07012 and 07013 appeared, were short-lived; leaving Hamworthy by 1977, they were withdrawn from BR service almost immediately.

Next to arrive on the scene were the standard BR 350 hp 0-6-0 shunting engines of class '09', Nos. 09024, 09025 and 09026 being transferred to Branksome depot. In late 1980 Branksome depot ceased to be responsible for maintenance of the shunters and the trio were transferred away. From then the shunting locomotive was supplied by Eastleigh depot, heralding the arrival of the first of the similar but lower geared, slower speed class '08s' in the shape of No. 08150. This engine's stay was short being replaced in January 1981 by No. 08845, this engine becoming something of a regular at Hamworthy working on and off until 1987. After travelling down to Hamworthy the engine remained for a number of weeks before being swopped. Initially the locomotive stabled at Branksome depot overnight travelling light engine daily to and from Hamworthy Goods. However, around the mid-1980s the engine went out from Branksome on Monday morning and stayed at Hamworthy all week, stabling adjacent to Poole Harbour Commissioners offices which afforded a degree of security. In 1983 both Nos. 09025 and 09026 came back to work on the branch for a short period, but in January 1990 No. 09025 returned and remained at

Class '07' 0-6-0 diesel shunters came to the Hamworthy Goods line in 1975 when displaced from Southampton docks. In this 1976 photograph No. 07010 is heading toward Hamworthy Junction with a trip freight for Poole goods yard. It has just passed the site of Lake Halt and is seen crossing Lake Road bridge.   *Jeff Anderson*

Class '07' diesel No. 07010 is crossing Ashmore Avenue adjacent to Hamworthy Park in 1976. The road came into being after the loss of the passenger service on the line and as such the gates were always hand-operated by the train crew.   *Jeff Anderson*

Hamworthy for the next 12 months. During this period she became a 'bit of a pet' and was awarded a hand-painted name 'Victory' and a fictitious 'HW' shed code. In addition to the five '08'/'09s' mentioned above, Nos. 08642, 08650, 08760, 08847, 08933, 09001, 09004 and 09015 also worked the branch.

Chapter Three chronicled the events surrounding the proposed closure of the Hamworthy branch in 1992. Whether it was by accident or design it was very apt that No. 09025 the Hamworthy 'pet' carried out the last BR shunting turn on Friday 8th May. The following week Poole Harbour Commissioners took over responsibility for the shunting duties using a Yorkshire Engine Co. 'Janus' type diesel-electric 0-6-0 named *Astolat* and bearing an ASW numberplate No. 391. This locomotive was on loan from ASW, *Astolat* remaining in use until November 1992 by which time PHC had located a locomotive of its own. This turned out to be a 4-wheeled diesel (Works No. 173V) built in 1966 by Thomas Hill Ltd (Rotherham). Before coming to Poole it underwent an overhaul emerging from works bearing a plate inscribed 'Yorkshire Engine Co. L116 re-worked 1993'; it remains in Poole on the books of PHC. Whilst this engine was in works the company loaned/hired a 4-wheeled Hibberd 'Planet' diesel No. 3958 of 1961 bearing number RS58. Originally built for the Hartley Quarry Co. in Cumbria it was later sold, after passing through the hands of several owners, by 1992 the locomotive had become a hire locomotive for the Yorkshire Engine Co. and spent some time at Cheriton, Kent involved in the construction of the Channel Tunnel. Following its stint at Poole it changed hands several times before being sold into preservation. It has recently been restored and can be found just a few miles from its original place of work at the Stainmore Railway Company, Kirkby Stephen East station, Cumbria.

Just three types of main line diesel worked on the line after 1967, they were the indigenous Southern class '33s', and the ubiquitous class '47s', plus as mentioned in Chapter Three the class '73' electro-diesels appeared a few times in 1982. Other visitors on an occasional basis were class '20s' Nos. 20901 and 20904 working the annual weedkilling train. Saturday 13th May, 1989 saw a new type of motive power to the line in the shape of class '37' No. 37230 which arrived to work an extra load of steel.

This heralded the end of regular class '47' workings from Hamworthy when on 15th May, 1989 No. 47283 departed with the steel train. Next day No. 37197 worked the steel, she was followed on the 17th by No. 37884, one of the refurbished, re-geared, heavyweight variants. In July 1989 No. 37905 *Vulcan Enterprise* put in an appearance as the first of the small '37/9' sub-group to visit the line, in due course all six (Nos. 37901-906) came to Hamworthy. The '37s' were nicknamed 'Growlers' due to the sound of their exhaust. These distinctive and charismatic machines remained in control of the steel trains, sometimes working in pairs, until February 1993.

Type '5' diesels then appeared in the shape of Cardiff (Canton)-based class '56s'. This 3,250 hp type had a short six months' stint working over the branch beginning with No. 56060 on 5th February and ending with No. 56076 on 24th September, 1993. The next working on 8th October saw one of the 3,100 hp class '60s' appear in the form of No. 60096 *Ben Macdui*, after that date the class '60s' worked the steel train consistently until its demise. Four years later in 1997, in conjunction with the contract to bring stone to the branch, two new diesel types appeared on the branch. These were the BR-built class '58s', No. 58035 being the

Hamworthy, New Quay. 'Janus' type Yorkshire Engine Co. diesel-mechanical 0-6-0 *Astolat* from Allied Steel & Co. Cardiff was loaned to Poole Harbour Commisioners from May to November 1992. The locomotive is seen on 4th September, 1992 alongside the PHC shed 'P' built on the site of Wood's/Corralls' Ballast Quay coal depot.   *Author*

Following the return of *Astolat* to Allied Steel & Wire, this 1961-built 'Planet' 4-wheeled shunter No RS58 was hired to Poole Harbour Commissioners by Yorkshire Engine Co. The locomotive arrived in Poole after a spell involved in construction work of the Channel Tunnel, it is now preserved at the Stainmore Railway Company, Kirkby Stephen. It worked the port area while the locomotive purchased by PHC was being overhauled.   *Author*

Seen heading for New Quay to load steel coil is the present Poole Harbour Commissioners (PHC) locomotive, it carries a plate worded 'Yorkshire Engine Co. L116 re-worked 1993'.

Author

In this view taken on 27th July, 1999 the PHC locomotive stands on Hamworthy, New Quay at the extremity of the Hamworthy branch as steel billets are loaded, Poole Town Quay is in the background. *Author*

After the demise of the class '07' shunters three BR class '09' 350 hp shunting locomotives Nos. 09024/025/026 were allocated to Bournemouth. The picture on page 75 depicts James Brothers Ltd fixed crane, when this fell into disrepair the company used a mobile crane on the loading dock to unload consignments of steel. On 29th December, 1979 the final load of structural steel consigned to them by rail is unloaded by James Bros' staff, with No. 09024 in attendance. *Author*

Class '09' No 09026 hauls a rake of empty wagons towards New Quay on 3rd March, 1983. They are to be loaded with steel coil. *Anthony E. Trood*

Hamworthy Junction signalman Alan Greatbatch prepares to hand the single line token to the secondman of class '33' locomotive No. 33 010 on 16th September, 1981. Class '33s' were a regular sight on the Hamworthy Goods line from the end of steam until 1989, after that date they made spasmodic appearances until 1997. *Terry Saunders*

Ashmore Avenue crossing, looking up the line toward Hamworthy Junction. On 2nd October, 1983 the travelling shunter attempted to hold back the gates in the teeth of a gale. Having called on the train headed by class '33' No. 33 112, the wind gained control blowing one gate back to become jammed between locomotive and first wagon! *Terry Saunders*

Class '47' locomotives also worked the Hamworthy branch and this unidentified example has just arrived with a load of coal for Corralls household coal facility on the old Railway Wharf. In the foreground of this early 1980s photograph work is in hand on the second phase of Poole Harbour Commissioners' new ferry terminal. The large boulders mark the spot where the old up platform once stood.   *Terry Saunders*

In 1993 class '56' locomotives had a brief spell working steel trains from Hamworthy to Cardiff. The first such occasion on 5th February, 1993 saw, appropriately enough, No 56060 *Cardiff Rod Mill* work the service as the steel was bound for that works.   *Author*

A bit of overkill on the Hamworthy branch ! Due to a shortfall of OBA wagons, Eastleigh depot rostered a 3,100 hp class '60' No 60090 *Quinag* to trip three extra empty wagons to Hamworthy Goods on 21st May, 2003.   *Author*

first, weighing 130 tonnes, these locomotives are the heaviest to have worked over the line. On 2nd July, 1997 the first of the American- and Canadian-built General Motors class '59s' appeared when No. 59101 powered the first stone train. Since then all the class '59s' working in the UK, including the ex-National Power class '59/2s', have worked to Hamworthy with stone from the Mendips.

Since the privatisation of BR two freight companies, Mendip Rail (MRL) and English, Welsh & Scottish (EWS) have worked trains to Hamworthy. This latter company began introducing 250 General Motors, Canadian-built 3,300 hp class '66s' in 1998, No. 66021 becoming the first of the type to work into Dorset and down the Hamworthy branch on 23rd November, 1998. Since then the '66s' have worked all of the commodities which pass over over the branch. Spanish-built General Motors 125 mph class '67s', originally built in 1999 for postal trains, first appeared on the Hamworthy branch in March 2004 'top & tailing' a Serco track inspection train. These track inspection trains had previously been worked by class '47s', a cyclical four-monthly diagram along the Weymouth line usually sees the Serco train visit the Furzebrook or Hamworthy branches on alternate trips.

There is of course one other type of occasional traffic over the line, and that is the carriage of passengers. Although there are many former passenger carrying lines in the UK which have been relegated to freight only use, the Hamworthy branch would seem to hold the record for its 110 years without regular passengers. If the few wartime months in 1917/1918 that it carried workers to Lake Halt is discounted, the branch carried regular passengers for just 49 years. Those 110

Class '59s' are the usual motive power for the Hamworthy stone trains. On 27th March, 2000 No. 59203 *Vale of Pickering* became the first class '59/2' to visit Dorset. Originally built in Canada in 1995 for National Power to haul power station coal trains in the North of England, it is seen arriving at Hamworthy Goods to run-round empty stone wagons before returning to the Mendips.   *Author*

Five stars on the front buffer beam denote the locomotive is No. 59005 *Kenneth J. Painter*. Adorned in Yeoman livery, No. 59005 is ready to depart Hamworthy Goods on 13th September, 1999 with stone empties.   *Paul Kneller*

On 28th December, 2007 class '66' No. 66232 arrives at Hamworthy Goods with empty wagons to collect a consignment of coiled sheet steel from the Poole Harbour Commissioners' stockpile. The loaded train departed after dark the next day, sadly, unless more traffic is won from roads this may well prove to be the last revenue-earning freight flow over the Hamworthy branch. It is to be hoped this is not the case.   *Author*

years of freight usage means it is rare track for the 'track bashers', those railway enthusiasts who choose to attempt to travel over all sections of the national network. Therefore like all other freight lines it attracts special trains carrying railway enthusiasts. The first of these specials ran on 7th June, 1958 and is illustrated on page 76, the full list of all known enthusiast specials is listed below:

Date	Motive Power	Tour Organiser
7.7.1958	'M7' class 0-4-4T No. 30107	Railway Enthusiasts' Club
25.8.1963	'M7' class 0-4-4T No. 30052	Southern Counties Touring Society
18.4.1964	'Q' class 0-6-0 No. 30548	Locomotive Club of Great Britain
16.10.1966	Class '4' 2-6-0 No. 76026 and class '3' 2-6-0 No. 77014	Locomotive Club of Great Britain
18.9.1971	Class '33' No. D6528 + 4TC No. 403	Poole Grammar School Railway Society
3.2.1973	Class '33' No 6511 + TC set	Locomotive Club of Great Britain
1.6.1974	Demu No. 1130	Stephenson Railway Society
10.10.1981	Demus Nos. 1110, 1130	Railway Correspondence & Travel Society and Southern Electric Group
19.3.1983	Demus 1017, 1032	Hertfordshire Rail Tours
7.5.1988	Class '33' No. 33103 + 4TCs	Malcolm Ellis
3.8.1988	Dmus Nos. 53638, 53200, 51325, 59482, 51310	Plymouth Railway Circle
29.12.1990	Class '33' No. 33118 + 4TCs No. 8001 and 5TC No. 8110	Network SouthEast
15.3.1992	Class '37s' Nos. 37902, 37227 and class '33' No. 33114	DC Tours & Network SouthEast
20.04.1992	Class '33' No. 33008 and class '37s' Nos. 37131, 37107	Hertfordshire Rail Tours
06.11.1993	Class '37s' Nos. 37405, 37377	Pathfinder Tours
15.04.2000	Class '66' No. 66059 and class '60' No. 60007	Pathfinder Tours
24.03.2001	Class '66s' Nos. 66222, 66194	Pathfinder Tours
20.10.2001	Class '73s' Nos. 73110, 73136 and class '58' No. 58047	Hertfordshire Rail Tours

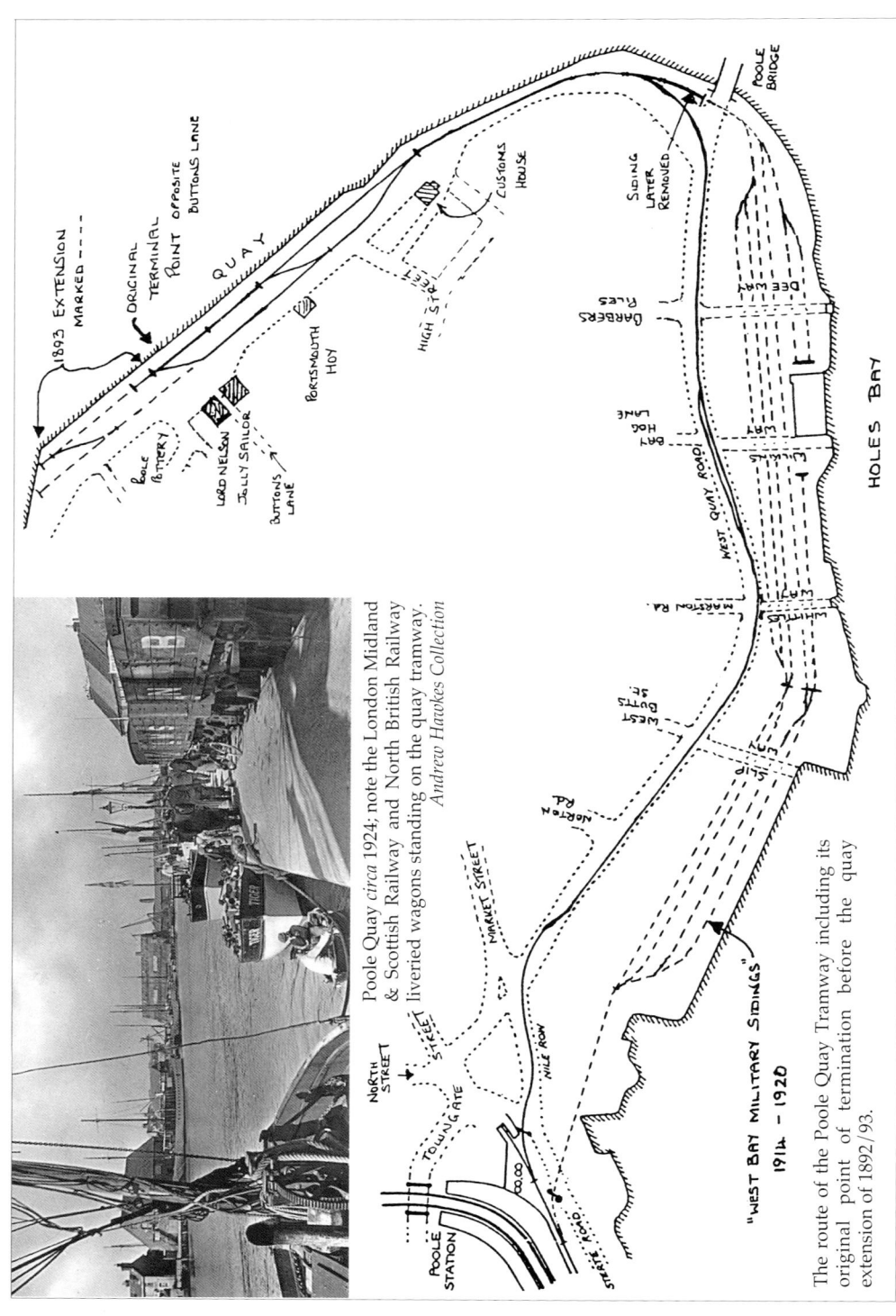

Poole Quay *circa* 1924; note the London Midland & Scottish Railway and North British Railway liveried wagons standing on the quay tramway.
Andrew Hawkes Collection

The route of the Poole Quay Tramway including its original point of termination before the quay extension of 1892/93.

1893 EXTENSION MARKED ----

ORIGINAL TERMINAL POINT OPPOSITE BUTTONS LANE

QUAY

CUSTOMS HOUSE

HIGH STREET

PORTSMOUTH HOY

LORD NELSON

JOLLY SAILOR

POOLE BATTERY

BUTTONS LANE

SIDING LATER REMOVED

POOLE BRIDGE

DEE WAY

BARBERS PILES

BAY HOG LANE

WEST QUAY ROAD

ILUM

WHITTLES

MARSTON RD

HOLES BAY

NORTON RD.

WEST BUTTS ST.

TUT DIP

MARKET STREET

NILE ROW

STREET

NORTH STREET

TOWNGATE

STRAND ROAD

00.00

POOLE STATION

"WEST BAY MILITARY SIDINGS" 1914 - 1920

Chapter Five

Poole Quay Tramway

This line began its life as an everyday part of the working scene in Poole, and after the initial opening the passage of a train probably caused no one to give it much more than a cursory glance. But by the 1950s, as one of the dwindling examples of street railways left in the country, it ended its days as a curiosity and a magnet for the growing band of railway photographers.

The proposed Poole & Bournemouth Railway, which was to bring the railway actually into the town of Poole as opposed to Hamworthy, had a clause included in the original Act of Parliament for a connecting line to Town Quay. The line from Broadstone was opened by the LSWR in December 1872. Eighteen months later in June 1874, after some prevarication with Poole Council who were pushing for the tramway to be built, the line to Town Quay had been laid and opened for traffic, giving connection to the growing national railway network and all the benefits this brought.

Classed as a street tramway, certain clauses governed the construction and working of the line. It was to be 'constructed upon the level of the streets and quays, so as not to obstruct the general traffic thereof'. From 1874 until the mid-1890s it was a single track throughout with two passing loops, only one of which was on the quay opposite the 'Jolly Sailor' public house where the line originally terminated. The doubling and additional section on the quay to make the full route length of 1 mile 14 chains (1 chain = 22 yds) came after the 1892/1893 quay extension eastward to what is now Fisherman's Dock; the map opposite shows its course, extent and final layout in the later years.

Leaving Poole station from the down bay platform the track left railway property via a gateway to cross Sterte Road, it then entered Nile Row to run down the middle of the street between houses and a timber yard. (All signs of this street are lost under the Poole end of the Holes Bay relief road.) From Nile Row the line entered West Quay Road and to ease the curvature around into this road the line crossed the street to the east (town) side, then recrossed to the west (Holes Bay) side of the street. It then remained on this west side as it progressed the full length of West Quay Road. One 'siding' in the form of a passing loop was provided on this section of line (between Dee Way and Whittles Way) for the use of the timber yards in this area.

At the lower end of West Quay Road on the approach to Poole lifting bridge the line again crossed the street as it turned its course to the east to run onto Poole Town Quay. A second passing loop was once located here, but around 1915 this layout was altered and part of the loop converted into a siding terminating adjacent to the (now) bridge engineer's house. The current public toilets, marine police office and lifeboat crew room now stand on the site.

On the quay proper the line remained restricted to a single track, lack of available road width precluded a second line until the Customs House was reached, at this point the greater width of quay and roadway allowed two tracks to run along the remainder of the quay. Three sets of crossover points

A postcard view of Poole Quay *circa* 1910 showing the tramway at the start of the double track section.   *Lens of Sutton*

Poole station in the 1950s; to the right of view in the down bay a wagon stands at the entrance to Poole Quay Tramway. This then proceeded along Nile Row marked by the advertising hoarding on the building wall.   *Lens of Sutton*

between the two lines were also provided, the operating handles for these points being contained in narrow recesses in the ground. To throw the points over, the handle, which was pivoted at the bottom end, was grasped and lifted to an angle of about 45 degrees until resistance was felt, a further, usually two-handed hard pull brought the lever upright and moved the points over, the handle was then released and dropped back into the recess below road level. In the early days all manner of goods and merchandise were carried on the line, if it had to go any great distance it went by train. Notable loads carried were pit props from Norway going to the local clay mines on the Isle of Purbeck and via the S&D to the Somerset coalfield in the Radstock area, some on occasions going even farther afield to the South Wales coal mines. A certain amount of rough sawn Baltic timber transhipped directly onto trucks on the quay, or from ship via a timber yard to rail wagons standing in the passing loop in West Quay Road, also went out on the tramway. At certain times, until the opening of the coal terminal at Hamworthy, household coal was brought in by ship for onward movement to goods yards and local coal merchants at wayside stations in Dorset and Hampshire.

Grain was another major import through Poole, some going to the local flour mills but other sacks and barrels were loaded into covered wagons for onward movement by rail; in early days, partly as protection against rats, most food items such as butter, biscuits, fresh or salted fish, etc. were transported in barrels. Whether barrels or boxes were used to transport the catches of the Poole fishing fleet to London during World War I is not known, but they almost invariably began their 113 mile journey on the quay line. As sailing ships gave way to steam-powered vessels an increasing amount of coal as fuel for ships was brought down the streets to the quay. This increase in coal traffic peaked in World War I when the Royal Navy used Poole as a major base. Other loads of coal at this time went to the extremity of the tramway to serve the town's gas works, which was situated on Poole quay on the site now occupied by the Quay Hotel.

Under normal circumstances coal for the gas works came in by ship and was off loaded by overhead gantry cranes, however, wartime conditions saw coastal shipping suspended. Hence the coal came in by rail and the tramway, but the wagons were still off-loaded by the gantry cranes. Later in 1923 when a new larger gas works was erected at a new location the old site became a coal stockpile point, coal transfer to the new works being in 'buckets' via an aerial ropeway. Traffic down the line was varied, but was mostly single wagon loads for the quay-based ships' chandlers and other local concerns such as Carter's Pottery (later Poole Pottery) and carried under the common carrier policy. But the majority of movements down the line were empty wagons to collect loads, although at certain times the grain flow was reversed and this commodity went out by ship from Poole. On the opening of the Royal Naval Cordite Factory at Holton Heath in 1916, until 1938 a major import through Poole for transport on the tramway *en route* to the factory was iron pyrites (fool's gold). The iron pyrites which came from San Telmo, Spain and Bjorkassen, Norway were used to produce sulphuric acid, about 20 tons of pyrites per day being required, equating to around 6,600 tons per year.

Class 'B4' 0-4-0T No. 30093 runs out from Nile Row and begins to traverse West Quay Road *en route* to the quay on the evening of 9th August, 1954. The photograph holds memories for the author as he spent 21 years working for Aish & Co. in the factory building seen in the background.   *Ivo Peters courtesy of Julian Peters*

'B4' class 0-4-0T No. 30087 is seen at the same location on 6th August, 1954 in the process of crossing West Quay Road from the east to west side and appears to be proving the old adage 'rules are made to be broken'. One rule of the tramway was 'The wagons must not be pushed, but drawn by the engine'; note the trail from 30087's cylinder cocks!

Ivo Peters courtesy of Julian Peters

A view of West Quay Road towards Poole station viewed from Poole lifting bridge approach. The tramway, clearly visible, had been closed for 3 months by the date of this photograph in July 1960.
H.C. Casserley

The former *St Malo*, 'B4' class No. 30093, is leaving Poole Quay in August 1954 heading onto the section of track seen in the photograph above. The car on the extreme right is coming off Poole lifting bridge.
Ivo Peters courtesy of Julian Peters

This August 1954 view of class 'B4' 0-4-0T No. 30093 departing from the quay has been published before, but it illustrates very well the flagmen that were required to walk ahead of the train to warn traffic of the train's approach.   *Ivo Peters courtesy of Julian Peters*

'B4' class No. 30093 is seen again on 18th April, 1953 halfway between Poole bridge and the Customs House on the single line section of the tramway. Across the water is Hamworthy; No. 30093 would have spent some of her day behind the buildings in view shunting the goods yard less than a ¼ of a mile away as the crow flies. But to reach Poole Quay old '93 would have travelled 5 miles.   *R. Gosling*

Unmistakably Poole, the Customs House is seen from the point where the single line becomes double for the remainder of its length along the quay. Note, lower right, the point handle in its recess and the removable wooden blocks which allowed access to the point mechanism. No doubt the curse of modern society, Health and Safety legislation, would not allow similar installations! *R.C. Riley/Transport Treasury*

On the same evening No. 30093 provides entertainment for visitors to the quay. During the 1950s the level of tourists on the quay began to rise causing problems for the train crew looking out for unwary pedestrians. On this spot a 'scrap iron structure', termed a sculpture now stands, the author, undoubtedly biased, would prefer to see the 'B4' at the position again.

R.C. Riley/Transport Treasury

On a glorious August 1954 evening class 'B4' 0-4-0T No. 30093 sets off for Poole station along Poole Quay with box vans in tow. Moored alongside the quay is the Paddle Steamer *Embassy*.
Ivo Peters courtesy Julian Peters

On the same evening further down the quay in the vicinity of the Lord Nelson and Jolly Sailor public houses, 'B4' No. 30093 waits with sizzling safety valves as the shunter secures one of the box van doors in readiness for departure. *Ivo Peters courtesy of Julian Peters*

A general view of Poole Quay in 1936 appears to have been taken from the roof of Poole Pottery. At least three colliers are tied up discharging coal or coke, the latter commodity was the usual load in the road vehicles with extended side boards. On the tramway tracks wagons of the Great Western, Southern and London Midland & Scottish railways are lined up. In the background across the channel is Ballast Quay coal yard. *Author's Collection*

This scene on Poole Quay depicts a rake of wagons being shunted between tracks near the extremity of the line on 18th April, 1953. *R. Gosling*

On the same date 'B4' class 0-4-0T No. 30093 is viewed alongside Poole Pottery whilst engaged in shunting coal wagons into position under the gas works coal unloading gantry.   *R. Gosling*

A view looking west along Poole Quay *circa* 1958, the photographer is almost at the extremity of the Quay and tramway.   *The Transport Treasury*

Above: Both gas works coal unloading gantries are viewed in this 1953 scene, the nearest is in the parked position with the extension arm raised. The other is gainfully employed unloading a ship, the transporter grab is positioned out on the lowered extension arm, over the vessel.

Author's Collection

Viewed looking west toward Poole station on 18th April, 1953 this view shows one of the gantries in use unloading railway wagons. The electric motors powering the bucket hoist and short traverse equipment were located in the enclosed section with the operator's cabin slung beneath it.

R. Gosling

After World War I a gradual decline in use of the line began with lorries taking some of the traffic, but it was still earning its keep and an asset to the port and again proved its worth during World War II. During this conflict the line saw heavy use, indeed in 1944 when the Americans arrived in Poole in the form of the US Army Transportation Corps, they used both road and rail from their supply base on Salisbury Plain.

In the build up to D-Day traffic levels reached an all time high, with vast amounts of petrol coming down the line. These highly flammable fuel trains demanded extra precautions such as accompanying outriders. The rule requiring all trains to be hauled along the line was rescinded for this cargo, as the locomotive propelled the tank wagons.

Also coming down the tramway in wartime for transfer onto BOAC flying boats were Red Cross parcels for British POWs. These parcels were flown initially to neutral Portugal, where from the capital Lisbon they eventually reached the POW camps. After the frantic activity of the war years it was back to normal on the railway and in the port. After Nationalisation of the railways in 1948 British Railways assumed responsibility for the line, trains now running twice daily and not as required as they had previously. These trains went down the line at 6.30 am and again 12 hours later at 6.30 pm; a round trip including shunting took between one to two hours.

Unfortunately rail traffic was still in decline because many ships were using New Quay at Hamworthy rather than Poole Town Quay, whilst those that still did discharged cargoes destined for local distribution, i.e. timber for Norton's Ltd or grain for Yeatman's and Christopher Hill's quayside grain stores. Coke was sometimes unloaded for movement to local rail-connected potteries but other cargoes discharged on the quay were either unsuitable for rail or went out on lorries, thus trains became shorter in length. The odd covered wagon was loaded or off-loaded by quay-based companies including Poole Pottery, but lorries soon began to make inroads into this traffic. A customer for much coal traffic during the Summer season had been the various paddle steamers that plied between Bournemouth-Swanage and the Isle of Wight. At various times some of the vessels had taken coal on the Hamworthy side, but usually it was from Poole Quay where, on return to Poole in the evening, these boats were re-fuelled ready for the next day. This dirty, dusty job was undertaken by a gang of men who shovelled the coal from the railway wagons into wicker baskets, these were then carried onto the ships to be tipped into their coal bunkers. Coal for these 'paddlers' came down the line in open wagons.

Following World War II the majority of the remaining steamers were converted to burn oil fuel, filling their bunkers either from an oil barge moored off Hamworthy or from road tankers on Poole Quay. The last coal burning paddle steamer was PS *Monarch* (1924), taking her last coal from railway wagons in September 1959. With the decline in rail traffic the decision was taken to close the line and therefore on 30th April, 1960 the last train traversed the tramway; officially it closed on 2nd May, 1960.

Over the next few months the lines were removed or covered over and by 1962 all traces were gone. No longer would cyclists fall off their machines as their wheels got stuck in the tracks or skidded on wet rails, no longer would young lads 'chase the train down the quay'.

Manning, Wardle 0-4-0ST, Works No. 594 of 1876, originally named *Pioneer*, later numbered 407 by the LSWR, became the first steam locomotive to traverse Poole Quay tramway in June 1899; it is seen here at Nine Elms.   *Norman Collection courtesy of the South Western Circle*

Vulcan an 0-4-0ST built in 1878 by Vulcan Foundry, Works No. 836, stands in the spur off the Poole Quay tramway at the rear of Poole station down platform buildings.   *Author's Collection*

Locomotives on the Tramway

From its opening date until 1899 the main source of motive power seems to have been horses hitched up to one or two wagons. It must be assumed that increased loadings prompted the trial of a steam locomotive in June 1899. For instance in 1894 180,000 tons of goods came through the Port of Poole from 1,350 ships. Not all would have been moved via the tramway as the Hamworthy branch would have handled a fair proportion of the tonnage, but the same report notes that on one occasion over 100 wagons were counted having been left standing on the tramway overnight! Mention has been made of the LSWR's involvement with docks, and to that end in 1881 they had purchased second-hand, two 0-4-0 saddle tanks built in 1876 by Manning, Wardle & Co. and set them to work in the Plymouth area including Sutton Harbour. Ten years later these engines were replaced, one locomotive was scrapped in 1892, but *Pioneer*, Works No. 594, later to be numbered 407 by the LSWR, survived working at Guildford and London before she was sent to Poole for the 1899 trial which proved successful.

From 9th August, 1899 steam was authorized to work the line, No. 407 (*Pioneer*) was joined by two identical 0-4-0ST engines built in 1878 by Vulcan Foundry of Newton-le-Willows, Works Nos. 836 and 837. The first bearing the LSWR No. 111 and named *Vulcan* arrived in April 1900 followed in May by LSWR No. 408 *Bretwalda* (Saxon for Britain's Ruler). *Bretwalda* remained in the area until 1903 when she was transferred to Winchester. A fourth locomotive also appeared in March 1901, this was an 0-4-0ST named *Ironside* built in 1890 by Hawthorn, Leslie; she received the number 458 in 1901. These last three locomotives had originally been built for the Southampton Dock Co., absorbed by the LSWR in 1892.

The trio, Nos. 111, 407 and 458, operated on the Quay line and at Hamworthy Goods, working from Hamworthy Junction shed up until 1904, when once again their roles were usurped by the type of locomotive that had ousted them from their previous Southampton Dock duties. These replacement locomotives were the class 'B4' 0-4-0 tank engines purpose-built for dock shunting. No. 94 of this type had made tests runs over the Quay line in October 1903. Various minor alterations to the track clearances in Nile Row and at other locations were necessary before they were allowed onto the line permanently, but by April 1904 the 'B4s' had arrived and here they stayed until the end in 1960. There is an unconfirmed report that consideration had first been given to using to ex-London, Brighton and South Coast Railway (LBSCR) class 'A', later to become class 'A1X', 0-6-0T locomotives on the line. Ex-LBSCR Nos. 646 and 668, renumbered by the LSWR to Nos. 734 and 735, were sent to Bournemouth in 1903. The report suggests a month's trial was envisaged; *if* the trial took place then it must be considered unsuccessful as no other engines of the type appeared. Nos. 734 and 735 then journeyed west in August 1903 to take up their appointed, but also unsuccessful, short-lived posts on the Lyme Regis branch.

At first only two 'B4s' were allocated, allowing *Vulcan* and *Ironside* to be moved away to be used on railway construction work, including strengthening the embankment at Pokesdown near Bournemouth. By May 1904 a third 'B4' had

Another 1878-built Vulcan Foundry locomotive, Works No. 837 *Bretwalda* was sister engine to *Vulcan* and spent some time in the early 1900s working the Poole Quay tramway.
W. Dunning/R.K. Blencowe Collection

Eastleigh on 14th April, 1922 and two ex-Poole Quay Tramway engines are seen together. Hawthorn, Leslie (Works No. 2174) of 1890, No. 734 *Clausentum* stands with No. 111 *Vulcan*. Both had originally been built for the Southampton Docks Co.   *H.C Casserley*

Hawthorn, Leslie 0-4-0ST *Ironside*, Works No. 2175, built in 1890 and seen in Southern Railway days at Nine Elms on 15th June, 1946 also worked the Poole Quay and Hamworthy branches. She was last in use on the line in 1944, a sister to *Clausentum*, both worked on construction work at Holton Heath in World War I.   *H.C. Casserley*

arrived, thus Nos. 88, 94 and 103 began the 56-year-association of the 'B4' type with the Poole area. No. 407 (*Pioneer*) was then moved on to be employed in the Woking area, she was working in London by 1906 and was on occasions hired out by the LSWR, at one time to Portsmouth Gas Works and later to Bournemouth Corporation. The reason for her use in Bournemouth is not known, but in all probability she was engaged in shunting the sidings of Bournemouth Tram depot which was connected to the LSWR at Bournemouth East Goods yard; she was out of use in 1919 and scrapped in 1921. *Vulcan* lasted until 1924 and was then sold, *Ironside* appears to have led a nomadic existence after 1908, regularly making visits to the area until 1923. In 1914 she was loaned to the contractors building the new Royal Naval Cordite Factory at Holton Heath.

The 'B4s' did not have things all to themselves, though, as the older engines returned to cover repairs, locomotive shortages and wartime contingencies. In 1906 an identical sister to *Ironside*, named *Clausentum* (the Roman name for Southampton) ex-Southampton Docks Co. No 457 (later renumbered 734), was noted in the area and made several appearances up until 1914 to cover just such occasions. *Clausentum* then also went on loan for construction works at the Cordite Factory at Holton Heath. During World War I No. 408 *Bretwalda* returned to Poole around mid-1914 and was noted in use at Hamworthy in 1916; she was withdrawn in 1924 and appears to have been replaced by our old friend No. 734 *Clausentum*. This engine is listed as transferred to the area in 1924, being quoted as: 'Bournemouth shed shunter/pilot and spare locomotive for Hamworthy and Poole Quay shunting'. After a short period at Guildford as shed pilot she was back in 1926 staying until 1927.

Built in Scotland by Shanks & Co., 0-4-0ST No. 108 *Cowes* is viewed at Nine Elms. This locomotive and sister No. 109 *Southampton* were both in Poole in 1910, No. 108 being noted 'derelict' at Hamworthy Junction whilst No. 109 was at work on Poole Quay. Both are real old relics from Southampton Docks, the pipes are an early form of condensing apparatus. *Norman Collection courtesy of the South Western Circle*

Two other 1876-built relics from Southampton Docks arrived in 1910 in the form of two Shanks Ltd tram engines, Nos. 108 *Cowes* and 109 *Southampton*. These Scottish-built engines had traversed streets before when working from Southampton main station to Royal Pier conveying passengers to the Isle of Wight ferry. Part of the Southampton Corporation agreement for street running was that they were fitted with an early form of condensing apparatus, thus they were adorned with large pipes which fed exhaust steam back into their water tanks.

When displaced from those duties No. 108 *Cowes* was hired or loaned during 1905-1906 to the Royal Engineers, Christchurch Bridge building depot, but by August 1910 she was noted dumped derelict at Hamworthy engine shed, so there is the possibility that she may have worked the Hamworthy and Poole quay lines. But No. 109 *Southampton* certainly did so, as the same report for August 1910 states she was working on Poole Quay. Both were withdrawn in 1913 and No. 109 is listed as sold to Kynoch's of Longparish in 1915, where she saw use in a Government wood distillation factory. No. 108 *Cowes* was also sold for £150, going of all places to a colliery at Haltwhistle, Northumberland.

The last of these 'old stagers', No. 734 *Clausentum*, left the area in 1927 when she needed heavy repairs, ending her days at Guildford in 1945. Apart from a couple of short visits by *Ironside* in the years up to 1944 as a 'repair cover engine', this left the class 'B4' in sole charge of Hamworthy Goods and Poole Quay shunting.

Bournemouth engine shed was the parent depot of locomotives outstationed at Hamworthy Junction sub-shed. In Southern Railway days class 'B4' 0-4-0T No. 92 is seen standing outside Bournemouth depot.   *B.L. Jackson Collection*

Dwarfed by 'Lord Nelson' No. 30862 *Lord Collingwood*, long time Poole Quay tramway engine 'B4' 0-4-0T No. 30093 is seen on Bournemouth depot soon after receiving an overhaul.
                                                                                   Alec Swain/Transport Treasury

The final duty on the Poole Quay line and at Hamworthy Goods undertaken by a class 'B4' was carried out by, now preserved, No. 30102 seen at Bournemouth depot on 31st March, 1960, a month before closure of the quay line.   *Author's Collection*

Another photograph of 'B4' class 0-4-0T No 30102 at Bournemouth depot, this view shows where the original, partially open cab, had been enclosed.   *Alec Swain/Transport Treasury*

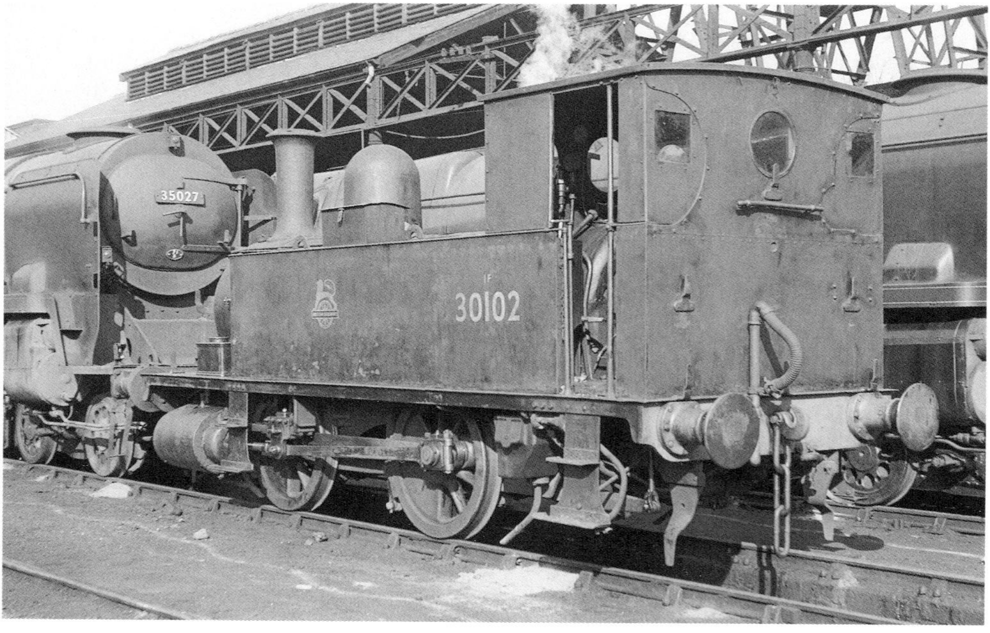

Working the Poole Quay Line

The class 'B4' locomotives were hardy little machines weighing 33 tons 9 cwt, with wheels of 3 ft 9¾ in. diameter and a wheelbase of 7 ft capable of negotiating a 4 chain radius curve. They were the engines on which most of the young firemen based at Bournemouth depot in the post-war years began their footplate careers, and retired Bournemouth driver Tom Upshall has related a couple of tales concerning his firing on the 'Poole Bug' as this turn was called.

After the closure of Hamworthy engine shed in 1954 the engine left Bournemouth locomotive depot at 6 am, and was allowed 17 minutes to reach Poole, where on arrival the crew would couple onto their train. Around 6.30 am they would set off for the Quay preceded by the obligatory flagman. One day in damp, drizzly conditions when rounding the curve from Nile Row to West Quay Road, Tom spotted the flagman waving his red flag. 'Whoa! Whoa!' shouted Tom to his driver because ahead square across the track was a milk float from the old Poole dairy firm of Tamplin's. As the wagons were only individually hand-braked the only means of stopping available was the hand brake on the engine. At the same time as shouting his warning Tom frantically wound on the brake handle, alas too late, the weight of train on wet slippery rails took control and pushed them with an almighty thump into the milk float; crates of milk flew into the road smashing bottles galore. The milkman reappeared and reluctantly moved the offending float; our gallant crew continued on their way leaving the hapless chap to clear up the mess as he cursed the railway and everything else in general. Next day they spotted the milk float, sporting a large round buffer dent on its rear end, judiciously parked on the other side of the street!

On another occasion as they approached the British Roadways depot at the lower end of West Quay Road they collided with a lorry as it pulled out into their path. It transpired that this was a brand new vehicle and so keen was the driver to get his new charge on the road he failed to see what was coming. However a quick check round revealed no major damage, so the 'B4' was put into reverse and moved back slightly. They had all failed to spot the locomotive's buffer hooked under the lorry's mudguard, result, one shiny new mudguard fell with a clatter into the street. Almost in tears the lorry driver wailed, 'Three years I've waited for a new vehicle, now look at it !'

Another tale concerns the habit of the crew of the returning morning service adjourning to a cafe situated in West Quay Road for breakfast, leaving the locomotive and train standing in the street. In former times this posed no problems but in the late 1950s road traffic levels were on the increase. One particular morning as Tom and his driver sat enjoying a cup of tea and a bacon sandwich the cafe door opened to reveal a policeman, and he addressed them thus: 'Get that bloody train moved or I will do you for obstructing the highway, and tell your mates if any of you stop here any more, we will book you'. So no more breakfasts, sadly times were changing, that increase in road traffic was yet another nail in the coffin for the street tramway.

Wagons on Poole quay tramway in 1953. *Above left:* Esso tank wagon No. 1710 adjacent to Esso's Poole depot in West Quay Road. *Above right:* Ex-LNER fruit van by Christopher Hill Ltd's No. 5 animal feedstuff store West Quay Road. *Below left:* A 13 ton coal wagon outside Christopher Hill's No. 4 store and Poole Foundry on Poole Quay. *Below right:* Ex-LSWR 10 ton van of 1905 vintage outside Poole Pottery on Poole Quay.

(All) *R. Gosling*

After the morning trip 'down the quay' the engine made its way to Hamworthy Goods where it shunted the goods yard and on to New Quay if required. It returned to Hamworthy Junction mid-afternoon, shunting there before departing for Poole to arrive at 6.17 pm for the evening trip to the quay. In the dark winter months courting couples sometimes parked across the track; if the car occupants were too preoccupied, the locomotive crew eased the 'B4' up as close as possible before hanging on the whistle. They then watched in amusement as the car driver struggled to move out of the way, luckily in the panic no one ever selected the wrong gear and shot forward over the quayside! This evening trip was prone to cause havoc in the summer time as unwary daytrippers sometimes left their cars parked across the track; this then needed the engine crew and several bystanders to 'bounce' the offending car out of the way.

As a consequence the tail end of the train sometimes blocked the road onto and off the lifting bridge and although road traffic was not at today's level it did cause a minor traffic jam. One other problem came when the wheels of the push-along barrows from which prawns and cockles were sold got stuck between the tracks, a hard tug usually got them out but sent the cockles flying! After shunting the quay the 'B4' negotiated West Quay Road once more as it returned to Poole station with any wagons collected on its foray, usually leaving them behind Poole signal box for the yard shunter to collect. The locomotive was booked light engine from Poole at 8.12 pm for a return run to Bournemouth, arrival here was supposed to be 20 minutes later at 8.32 pm. However, it was done in less by some drivers when a bus needed to be caught, or a pint in the local was on the cards! The gyrations of one of these engines out on the main line whilst going at speed, light engine, had to be seen to be believed! Luckily the final years attracted a few photographers who recorded the trains in action. At least the last few years of the 'B4s' on the quay are preserved in pictures, but those Poole citizens under about 45 years of age can only guess at the sight and sound those delightful locomotives made as they slowly clanked and hissed their way along the quay.

Of the 25 members of the 'B4' class, at least 12 are known to have worked the quay line, Nos. 83, 86, 87, 88, 91, 92, 93, 94, 99, 100, 102, and 103. In 1948 to identify ex-Southern Railway locomotives, British Railways added 30,000 to these numbers, the last engines to see service on the quay under BR were thus:

30092: withdrawn from Bournemouth April 1949

30099: withdrawn from Bournemouth February 1949

30100: withdrawn from Bournemouth February 1949

30086: arrived Bournemouth February 1949, transferred to Dover, April 1954

30087: arrived Bournemouth July 1949, withdrawn from Bournemouth, December 1958

30093: arrived Bournemouth, from Southampton Docks, December 1947

30102: arrived Bournemouth, from Plymouth via a three month period of store, December 1958

No. 30093 arrived in the last month of the Southern Railway's existence as No. 93 bearing the name *St Malo*. She became the engine most associated with the quay line, being photographed many times. She was unfortunately moved

A view looking up West Quay Road towards Poole station showing a box van standing on the tramway, outside Christopher Hill's No. 5 store.   *R. Gosling*

away to work at Winchester in February 1960 and was withdrawn from service at the end of March 1960, thus it fell to No. 30102 to work the last train on 30th April, 1960. No. 30102 then went to Eastleigh leaving Bournemouth for the last time on 26th May, although BR officialdom took 18 months to issue a transfer notice on 9th November, 1961!

During this time No. 30102 returned to the old 'B4' haunts in Southampton Docks, being noted there in November and December 1960 and again in July 1961. She remained in use with BR until withdrawn from service in September 1963. In 1964 Butlin's bought the locomotive and had it restored to 1920s condition complete with its old name *Granville*. It then went for display as a children's attraction at Skegness Holiday camp alongside ex-London Midland & Scottish Railway No. 6100 *Royal Scot*. In 1971 it was moved again to Bressingham Steam Museum, Norfolk as a non-working exhibit and is still there, the only remaining and most tangible relic of the days of the Poole Quay Tramway.

Poole Tramway

This is a single line about one mile in length, connected with the Down Goods Siding at Poole Station, and terminating at the Quay. It is worked by a steam Locomotive and is for Goods traffic only.

The speed of Engines and Trains must not, under any circumstances exceed FOUR miles an hour, and on every occasion a man must walk about 20 yards in advance of the Engine, carrying red and green flags, and a red light at night, in order to warn the public of the approach of the Engine or Train, and, if occasion should demand, signal the Driver to stop.

The load of the Train must not exceed 25 loaded Wagons from the Quay to the Station, and 30 empty Wagons from the Station to the Quay.

The Wagons must not be pushed, but drawn by the Engine.

Extract from instructions for working the Poole Quay Tramway.

Chapter Six

They Also Served

During World War I in 1914 a large tract of land known locally in Poole as West Shore bordering the shores of Holes Bay was taken over by the military. Poole at the time was in use as a Naval base and the land was required for stores purposes; late in 1914 and continuing into early 1915 the military laid a network of sidings on this land (*see map p. 128*). The sidings which received the name West Bay Military Sidings extended the full length of the foreshore running parallel with the Poole Quay Tramway and West Quay Road.

During a visit to Poole Museum in 1995 the author, in company with a member of the museum staff, investigated old maps of the area and wrongly assumed that buildings on the site would have precluded the tracks extending the whole length of the foreshore. The stark reality was that the original structures shown on the maps, mainly timber stores and other timber yard buildings, were arbitrarily demolished. Thus was the power of the state in wartime, those buildings that survived this treatment were used as food stores by the RASC.

This network of lines was connected to the national railway system via a connection in the down bay line at Poole station, which crossed Sterte Road close to the quay tramway connection into Nile Row. A second connection was made to the Poole Quay tramway near to Poole lifting bridge. It would appear that at least two locomotives worked within the site, the first being a Hudswell, Clarke locomotive named *Pioneer* requisitioned in 1914 from Poole-based pottery company Sharp, Jones Ltd. A further reference indicates that the other locomotive (also requisitioned) was Somerset & Dorset Railway 0-4-0T No. 26A which usually saw use in the Radstock area. After being used at Poole, the engine was transferred to spend a period working at Holton Heath Royal Naval Cordite factory. This engine was one of those nicknamed 'Dazzlers' due to their usual pristine condition, it was constructed at the S&D's Highbridge works in 1895.

The Poole persons and traders who had forfeited their land and business premises, being patriotic citizens, accepted the situation during the war years. However, after the war in 1919 when the authorities failed to show signs of vacating the site, they became vociferous in demanding action. The War Office had in June of that year offered the site to Poole Harbour Board and Poole Town Council, both of whom declined as did the LSWR. On 1st September, 1919 the site was then offered to the Ministry of Transport; it was all this prevaricating with their livelihood that caused the timber merchants and traders to protest. They had been paid no compensation or rent, and were constantly having to turn shipping and business away.

At last toward the end of September a train of box vans appeared and a start was made on removing the 10,000 tons of stores still on site. Finally in January 1920 with the site cleared the rails and connections were removed. The land was handed back to the original occupiers and the sidings became one of the shortest-lived rail connections to Poole Harbour.

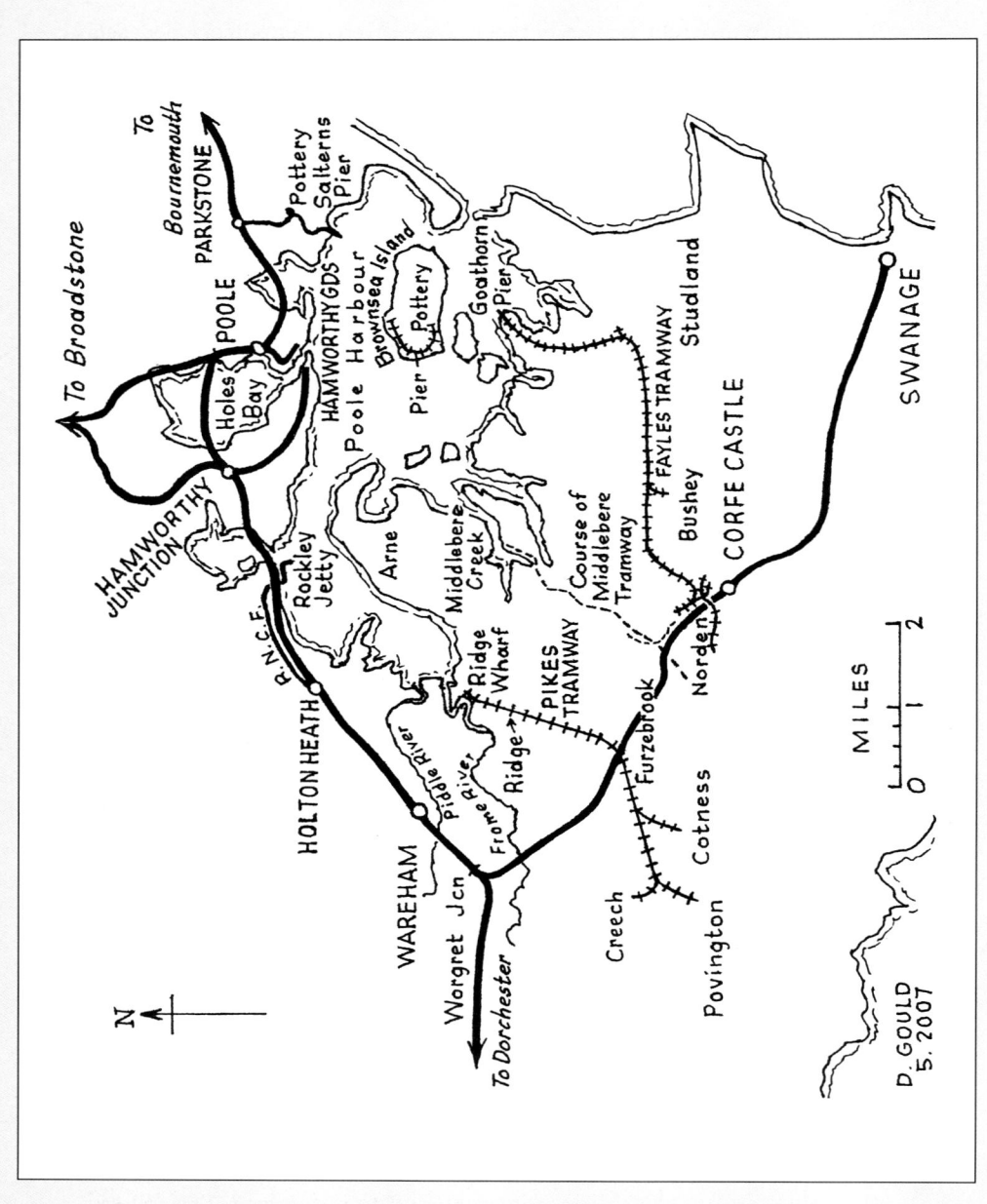

N

To Broadstone

To Bournemouth

PARKSTONE

Pottery
Salterns Pier

POOLE

Holes
Bay

HAMWORTHY GDS

HAMWORTHY

Poole Harbour

Brownsea Island

Pier
Pottery

Goathorn
Pier

FAYLES TRAMWAY

Studland

HAMWORTHY
JUNCTION

Rockley
Jetty

R.N.C.F.

Arne

Pier

Middlebere
Creek

Course of
Middlebere
Tramway

Bushey

CORFE CASTLE

SWANAGE

HOLTON HEATH

Ridge
Wharf

Ridge→

PIKES
TRAMWAY

Furzebrook

Norden

Piddle River

Frome River

WAREHAM

Worgret Jcn

To Dorchester

Creech

Cotness

Povington

MILES

0   1   2

D. GOULD
5. 2007

It may not be generally known but there were seven other points where sets of rails provided connection to the waters of Poole Harbour, six directly, the seventh indirectly, this system being the earliest built will be described first.

Pike's Tramway as it was known is reputed to have been opened in 1840 by the company of Pike Bros, it ran entirely on the Isle of Purbeck as a narrow gauge line listed by the Industrial Railway Society as 2 ft 8 in. gauge, although some publications list the system dimension as being of 2 ft 8½ in. Its route was from clay mines near Furzebrook (between Wareham and Corfe Castle) to Ridge Wharf on the River Frome (Wareham River). It was constructed in a more or less straight line on a gently falling gradient from the mine to the wharf allowing gravity working to be used, i.e. the loaded clay wagons rolled downhill under the control of a brakesman all the way to Ridge.

Here the clay was loaded into barges, empty wagons were then drawn back to the mine by horses (they got a free ride downhill in special horse-carrying wagons). When in 1866 the company extended the line inland from Furzebrook to new clay diggings they introduced steam traction in the form of a locomotive they named *Primus*, the Latin for No. 1, next came *Secundus* and so on until their seventh and final locomotive in 1930 became *Septimus*.

In 1868 a second Purbeck clay mining company, Fayle & Co., opened a mile-long line from Newton Heath on the southern shores of Poole Harbour to Goathorn point (opposite the southern shore of Brownsea Island). This line was later extended to Norden, adjacent to Corfe Castle, a total distance of 5¾ miles on a gauge of 3 ft 9 in. Their first steam locomotive was built in Poole by Stephen Lewin's South Road-based Poole Foundry in 1870.

At Goathorn Fayle's constructed a short pier onto which the rails extended, at the end of this pier was a chute which could be raised and lowered like a drawbridge, the clay being tipped down the chute into barges. These clay barges, and those from Ridge Wharf, were then towed by tugs around to Poole and Hamworthy Quays (Railway Wharf), where the clay was transhipped to larger sea-going vessels for onward movement to the Staffordshire potteries.

It should be pointed out that both these narrow gauge systems, and in particular Fayle's railway, superseded a horse-worked plateway which also connected to a Poole Harbour creek. It was built in 1806 by Benjamin Fayle and ran 3½ miles from the Norden clay pits to Middlebere Creek. Wagons with ordinary non-flanged wheels were towed along a set route guided by L-shaped upright (plates). Little is known of this system which is thought to have fallen into disuse around 1885/1890; although not a railway in the true sense, mention is made here for interest, and historical accuracy.

It has been reported that in 1914 Pike Bros sent out 28,000 tons of clay by ship whilst Fayle's dispatched 18,000 tons. This trade through Poole via the two tramways began to decline as more and more clay went directly onto trains at interchange sidings which both companies had on the Swanage branch line. By 1937 both tramways saw little or no traffic to their seaborne outlets, indeed Goathorn Pier was destroyed in 1940 to prevent any wartime German invasion force using it.

The only workings the lines saw were to and from the main line railway sidings; Pike's system closed in 1965 whilst a short length of Fayle's system,

A general view of Pike Brothers engine shed and workshop in April 1956. The former line to Ridge Wharf went off to the right of picture. Pike Bros amalgamated with Fayle and Co. in 1949.
Roger Holmes (Photos from the Fifties)

The transhipment shed at Furzebrook April 1956. This facility on the former LSWR line to Swanage led to the demise of clay transportation through the Port of Poole via the narrow gauge line to Ridge Wharf.   *Roger Holmes (Photos from the Fifties)*

The rebuilt Pike's locomotive *Tertius* seen in 1955 at Furzebrook. Originally built by Manning, Wardle in 1886, Works No. 999, she was given this 'top heavy' look in 1951 when she received the boiler of Fayle & Co's Poole-built locomotive *Tiny*. A classic case of the Dorset 'make do and mend' policy, when it was found the firebox would not fit between the frames it was simply perched on top! *Roger Holmes (Photos from the Fifties)*

May 1955 at Furzebrook, on the left we see the rear end of *Tertius* and its 'double glazed' apparently convertible cab. On the right *Sextus* is viewed head on.

(Both) Roger Holmes (Photos from the Fifties)

A broadside view of *Quintus* at Furzebrook in 1955.   *Roger Holmes (Photos from the Fifties)*

Pike Brothers 2 ft 8½ in. gauge locomotive *Quintus*, a Manning, Wardle 0-4-0ST, Works No. 1854 built in 1914, rebuilt in 1934. She is seen at Furzebrook in April 1956.

Roger Holmes (Photos from the Fifties)

Pike Brothers locomotive *Sextus* a 1925-built Peckett 0-4-2ST, Works No. 1692, at Furzebrook in 1955. Note the standard gauge wagons in the background in a siding alongside the Swanage branch.   *Roger Holmes (Photos from the Fifties)*

May 1955 and *Sextus* is viewed from the left-hand side.   *Roger Holmes (Photos from the Fifties)*

Pike Brothers tramway end-tipping clay wagons Nos. 67 and 108 outside Furzebrook works freshly overhauled in 1955.   *Roger Holmes (Photos from the Fifties)*

A Pike's end-tipping wagon in raised position revealing the running gear. Note the tools on the framing indicating some delicate adjustments are being made.

Roger Holmes (Photos from the Fifties)

Fayle's two 3 ft 9 in. gauge locomotives are seen together at Norden awaiting disposal in 1948 after the remains of Fayle's system had been converted to 1 ft 11½ in. gauge. Nearest the camera is *Thames* a 1902-built Manning, Wardle 0-4-0ST Works No. 1552. Behind it the Poole-built 0-4-0T Lewin engine *Tiny* is seen with its 'winter cab' in position. Both locomotives would once have traversed Rails to Poole Harbour at Goathorn.

Author's Collection

which in 1948 had been rationalised and converted to 1 ft 11½ in. gauge, remained in use near Corfe Castle until 1971.

Both Pike's and Fayle's systems, including the Middlebere Plateway, are described in greater detail in the definitive publication by R.W. Kidner *The Railways of Purbeck* (Locomotion Papers No. 68 Oakwood Press). By coincidence, the pier at Goathorn was almost opposite one terminus point of a mile-long narrow gauge railway constructed on Brownsea Island in the early 1850s by the Branksea Clay & Pottery Co. This line was built in the shape of a large 'C', and ran from the pottery works built on Brownsea's south shore and followed the shore line around the island's western end to a clay pit on the north shore. This company was run by a dubious character named Colonel W.P. Waugh who had bought Brownsea Island in 1852 under the impression that the island clay seam was of sufficiently high quality to make porcelain. When it became apparent that the clay was of lower grade, it is claimed that he made fraudulent and inflated claims as to the size of the clay seam on the island. In 1856, when the fortunes of the pottery company were in financial turmoil, he did a proverbial 'moonlight flit' fleeing the country to Spain before being declared a bankrupt in 1857.

The pottery continued in use employing some of the 240 or so inhabitants of Brownsea until 1877, when it was run down and closed. Its connection to the sea was 'a substantial pier' onto which the railway ran to transfer the pottery products to ships. Coal/coke for the kilns came ashore via this pier, the railway was in all probability horse-worked as no evidence exists regarding steam working.

Fayle's first locomotive *Tiny* an 0-4-0T was built in Poole at Stephen Lewin's South Road Foundry about 1870. The engine is seen in 'summer mode' with upper section of its cab removed. When in 1948 the remaining working section of Fayle's line was re-gauged *Tiny*'s boiler was donated to Pike Brothers locomotive *Tertius* (*see page 157*).　　　*R.W. Kidner*

Fayle's railway at Norden after conversion to 1ft 11½ in. gauge is the setting of this 1953 photograph where ex-Welsh Highland Railway 2-6-2T *Russell* is in action. The area is now part of the preserved Swanage Railway park and ride station. Narrow gauge track is set to be relaid here as part of the Purbeck Mineral and Mining Museum.　　　*Roger Holmes (Photos from the Fifties)*

Left: Fayle & Co. 3 ft 9 in. gauge rails at Goathorn pier in 1938, the loading chute by which clay was loaded into barges for shipment to Railway Wharf at Hamworthy is seen raised, with Brownsea Island in the background.

R.W. Kidner

Russell is seen in derelict condition in the background of this 1955 photograph during a railway enthusiast's visit, in the foreground are some 4-wheeled clay carrying skips.

Roger Holmes (Photos of the Fifties)

After *Russell* arrived in Dorset in 1948 problems with the leading pony truck saw its removal, after which it ran as an 0-6-2T. The locomotive is seen heading a load of clay at a date prior to its withdrawal from service in August 1953 due to boiler problems.

Roger Holmes (Photos from the Fifties)

A map of the Parkstone and Lilliput areas of Poole reveals the South Western Pottery line running from Parkstone station to the pottery and then to Salterns pier.

Reproduced from the 6 in., 1926 Ordnance Survey Map

A similar horse- or manpower-worked system just fulfils the railway connection to Poole Harbour criteria. A short ½ mile system of an undetermined narrow gauge operated from *circa* 1870 until *circa* 1928 in the Lake area of Hamworthy, connecting clay pits to Lake Clay Works before continuing on to Lake pier. Clay excavated from the diggings was transported the short distance to drying sheds, from which a further set of rails went out onto the pier. Here the clay was transferred to barges or ships for onward movement in similar vein to the clay from Pike's and Fayle's systems.

Unlike the previous railway lines, two of the three remaining sets of rails to the harbour were of standard gauge (4 ft 8½ in.). The first was from the large George Jennings, South Western Pottery that once existed at the end of Pottery Road in the Lower Parkstone area of Poole. The extensive Conifer Park housing estate now covers the pottery site where street names such as South Western Way, Potters Way, Jennings Road and Crawshaw Road perpetuate the memory of the area's former use (Jennings and Crawshaw being prominent figures of the pottery company).

Researching dates for the early days of the pottery rail connection to the sea has produced something of a conundrum for the author, as varying reports of its history have been published. What is known for certain is that a standard gauge railway connection was made from the pottery works to Poole Harbour at Salterns Pier in the area of Poole known as Lilliput. The exact date is at present unknown, but in all probability it was laid in the year 1874, other confirmed facts are as follows:

1. The pottery was opened in 1856 by George Jennings & Co. and that clay was brought to the pottery by a horse-worked narrow gauge system.
2. Late in 1866 Jennings applied to the Board of Trade for permission to build a pier at Salterns which he claimed would free him from paying harbour dues; with permission granted construction of the pier was completed in 1867.
3. The kilns of the pottery were coal fired and reference is made in a book on Poole's history thus: 'Coal was once brought to the pottery from Salterns Pier by a light railway'.
4. It is also known from a later description by the Poole Archaeological Group that the rails on the pier were of 'narrow gauge'.
5. Finally in 1872 George Jennings & Company bought a brand new standard gauge 0-4-0 saddle tank locomotive (Works No. 159) from Fox, Walker of Bristol.

This year of purchase coincided with the opening of the direct railway connection into Poole (December 1872) and although it had been proposed as early as 1865 to extend the line east to Bournemouth, this extension to Bournemouth West was not forthcoming until 15th June, 1874. Once this line had its routeing finalised and had been built, the pottery then wasted no time in connecting itself to the national system. It did this by building a steeply-graded standard gauge line northward for about ¾ mile to the then one intermediate station on the new route at Parkstone. This pottery line was completed toward the latter end of 1874, the actual connection being made in the station goods yard on the south side of the main line. The pottery could now employ its expensive asset in the shape of the Fox, Walker locomotive which in

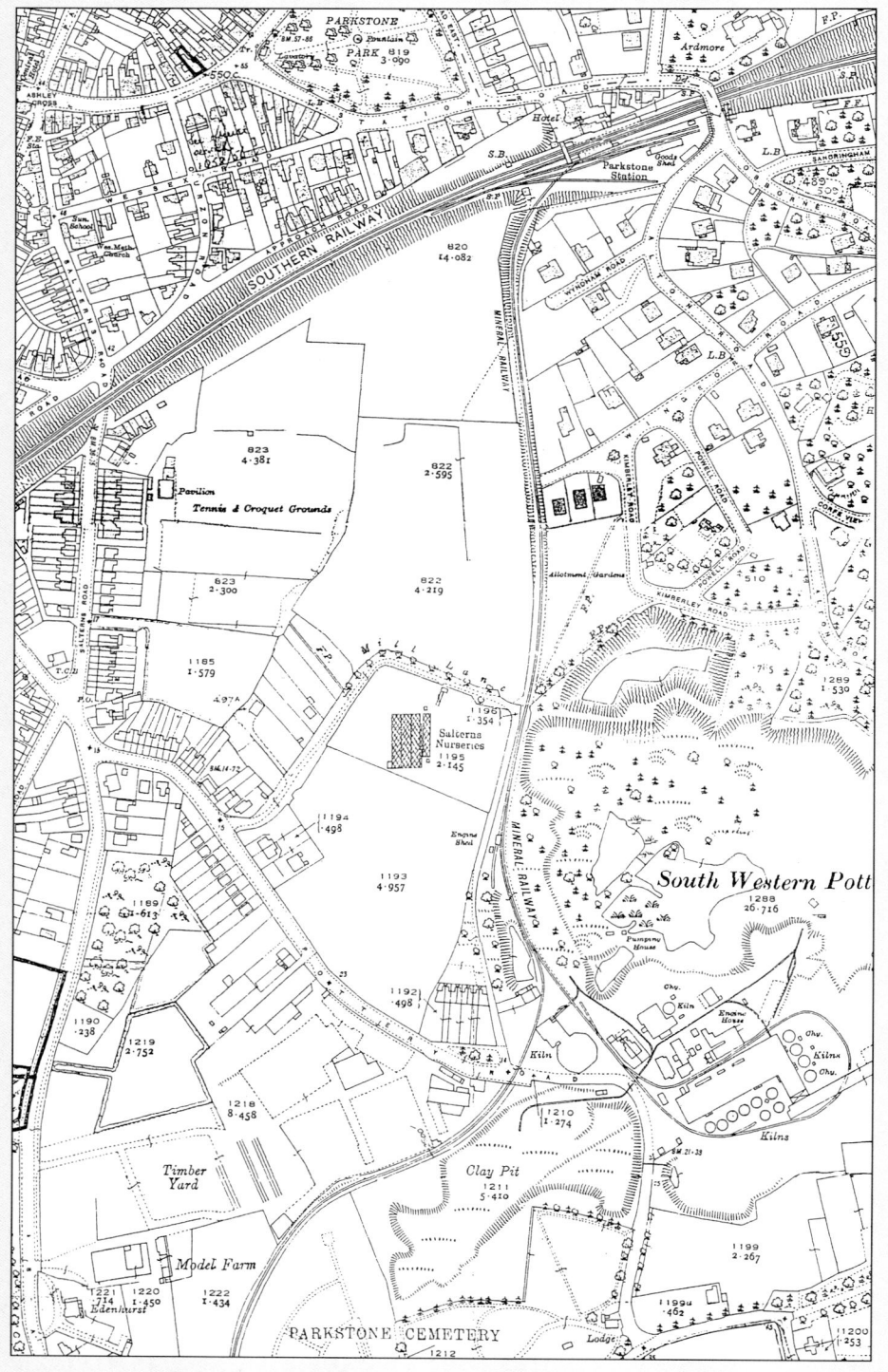

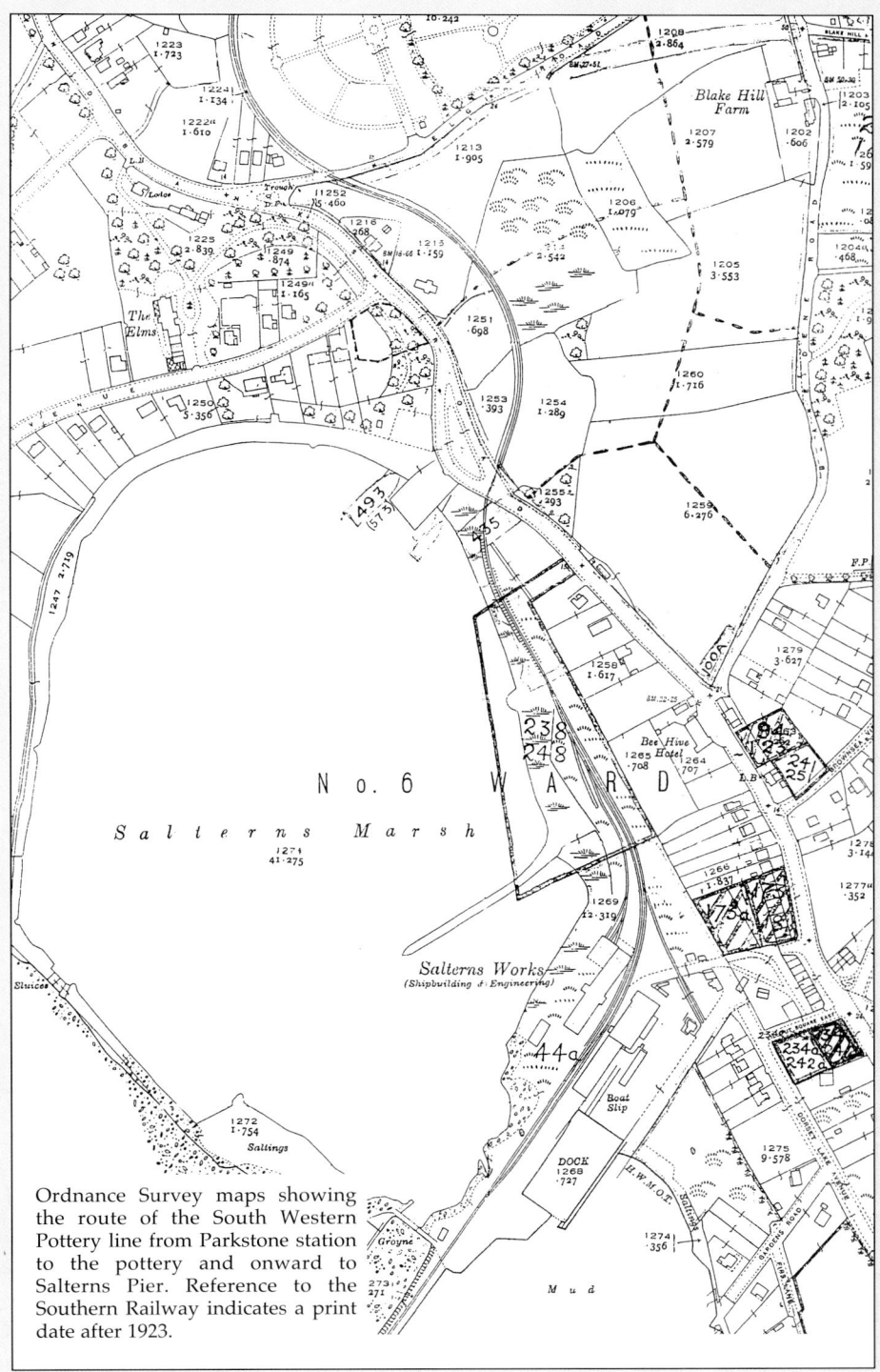

Ordnance Survey maps showing the route of the South Western Pottery line from Parkstone station to the pottery and onward to Salterns Pier. Reference to the Southern Railway indicates a print date after 1923.

A scene looking inland from Salterns pier, this undated view shows the track from South Western Pottery in a poor state of repair, indicating disuse for some time.

Andrew Hawkes Collection

In 1919 a share Prospectus for a proposed company 'Salterns Limited' contained this image, the only known photograph of *George Jennings* on the Salterns Pier section of the pottery railway. The factory chimney in both photographs gives a reference point.

Author's Collection courtesy of Robin Moy

theory it could not have used for at least 16 months! At this point conjecture plays a major part as exact chronology is somewhat hazy, but by amalgamating the known facts and some anecdotal tales from an ex-employee, the following seems to the most probable explanation?

It has been stated by some that the standard gauge route to Salterns Pier was not laid and opened until *after* 1902, only to be abandoned when a second standard gauge line was laid to the same point, i.e. Salterns, via a different route at an even later date! This would seem highly unlikely, most probably *two* slightly varying routes were indeed laid to Salterns Pier, but the first was an extension of the clay pit narrow gauge system laid *circa* 1866/7 to run out onto the then new pier for the coal to be brought in and finished products to go out. One unofficial and unsubstantiated document in local circulation indicates a gauge of 51 inches (4 ft 3 in.) for the narrow gauge!

George Jennings' origins were in London where they still maintained and operated premises. Their London address was given as Palace Wharf, Stangate, London, SE indicating that most likely shipments to London were, in early pre-rail days, by sailing barges to said Palace Wharf.

Thus construction of the pier obviated the need for a 3½ mile horse and cart delivery run over mainly rough tracks from Poole Quay and/or the railway at Hamworthy to the pottery and vice versa. In the early 1870s Jennings and the Port of Poole were engaged in a legal wrangle over harbour fees; Jennings considered he was exempt from these charges as Salterns Pier was the pottery's responsibility. Ships manifests of 1868 and 1869 being quoted in evidence show pipes going out and coal in quantities of up to 200 tons coming in (Jennings lost the case in 1873 and had to pay £2,789 in back harbour dues and costs etc.). That such large quantities of coal were taken along a narrow gauge line constructed solely on the pier to be tipped into horse and carts for short haul transportation into the pottery as some suggest, while feasible, is also unlikely. The logical conclusion is that the pier's narrow gauge rails were connected to those already existing in the pottery area. At a later date, between 1872 on purchase of the Fox, Walker locomotive and by 1890 at the very latest, the second set of rails, i.e. the standard gauge line, was laid to Salterns Pier on a route which varied slightly on exit from the pottery to avoid a proposed cemetery. This route after the deviation rejoined the route of the narrow gauge line. This was then regauged to standard gauge and at this gauge it is known to have continued only as far as the landward end of the pier.

Salterns Pier was built of old pipe and brick rubble at the landward end and of timber out into the shipping channel; most probably it was of insufficient strength or proportions to support the wider new line, thus the old narrow gauge was retained on the pier. An indication that the standard gauge track to the pier was laid in 1874 at the same time as the link to Parkstone station is alluded to in another quote in a local history book concerning pottery products thus: 'Their universal use was such that it warranted extension of the railway from Parkstone station to the works *and also* from the pottery to Salterns Pier from which they were exported'.

This standard gauge route went south out of the pottery premises, skirted the western perimeter of Parkstone cemetery (the old trackbed here is now tarred

Peckett *George Jennings* stands outside the South Western Pottery at Lower Parkstone, Poole on
30th April, 1957.   *Austin Attewell (Photos from the Fifties)*

A shot of *George Jennings* in his usual immaculate condition as he toys with one steel-bodied
mineral wagon at South Western Pottery.   *J.T. Rendell/Transport Treasury*

Another classic study of the British make do and mend policy *Q*. What do you do if your engine won't fit in the shed? *A*. Make the shed fit the engine! Note part of the end gable cut out to allow the dome and chimney to pass under, whilst odd bits of wood have been nailed to the doors to 'Bung up the 'ole'. Peckett *George Jennings* simmers partly outside his engine shed which was situated away from the main pottery buildings to the west of the line to Parkstone station (*see map page 166*). *Tony Legg Collection*

The third pit where clay was dug for the pottery, in contrast to the first two, was located on the opposite side of the standard gauge line. The 2 ft narrow gauge line reached the pit by means of this diamond crossing, ahead is the pottery and to the rear (*left*) Parkstone station, (*right*) clay pit. *Tony Legg Collection*

Looking down the pottery line from near Parkstone station, *George Jennings* can be seen in the distance running light to the pottery on 3rd July, 1961.   *H.C. Casserley*

On the same date *George Jennings* is seen on the approach to Parkstone station goods yard with one empty mineral wagon in tow. By this time traffic levels for the pottery line were well in decline.   *H.C. Casserley*

over and leads to Elgin Road water pumping station). From here the line crossed Sandbanks Road, then a rough track, it then ran along the harbour shoreline (in later years as the area developed this was at the rear of houses and the recently demolished Beehive Hotel). The line then passed through Salterns engineering works premises and out to the land end of Salterns Pier, in the vicinity of the present yacht club in Salterns Road about ¾ mile from the pottery.

As coal for the kilns now arrived via the main line and pottery spur, only outgoing goods, mainly the pottery's salt-glazed stoneware pipes for export, appear to have been transhipped between the two gauges. This was alluded to by the author's great uncle who was employed by Thomas Wragg (they took over George Jennings Ltd in 1903) for 58 years from 1901 until 1959 when he retired aged 72. He stated, 'When I started the engine only used to take trucks of pipes down to the "Blue Lagoon"', i.e. Salterns Pier.

The pottery was considered a leader in its field and exports were high with a considerable amount of its products finding their way to South America. The standard gauge line to the pier also saw the passage of wagons going to the Salterns works referred to above. In July 1918 this works was purchased by Alban, Richards Co. to repair railway wagons for, 'one of the great railway companies'. The use of Salterns pier declined after World War I, and although the line was still in place in 1922 it is doubtful if it was used much after 1925, if at all, and by 1935 the rails had been removed. Indeed there is one reference indicating its disuse as early as 1922; a map dated 1911 used by a Poole Council employee in 1922 to mark in new rateable properties in the Salterns area has the railway route pencilled on it in his own hand and annotated 'Disused Railway'.

This highlights the validity of using old maps to substantiate the route of old industrial railways as the line was definitely *in situ* in 1911 but had been omitted when the map was drawn up! A study of the 1919 Ordnance Survey map on page 4 supports this argument, again only the link to the main line is shown. However the photograph reproduced on Page 168 proves that the line was indeed in place as it was taken in 1919 to promote a new company share issue. One map dated 1902 shows what appears at first sight to be two narrow gauge lines going into the original clay pit, but a Poole Museum photograph of *circa* 1900 of the same site reveals these lines to be two standard gauge tracks with the narrow gauge at a higher level. This suggests that the narrow gauge was not included on early maps and would explain the lack of substantiated evidence of it continuing to Salterns Pier.

This photograph also shows standard gauge wagons being loaded with clay suggesting that the company sent out some of their clay via the standard gauge link, possibly to other works in the group or for sale to third parties. Steam locomotives always worked the standard gauge line; from 1874 the aforementioned 0-4-0 Fox, Walker was employed, being sold in 1893, when another 0-4-0 saddle tank was purchased new from Bristol this time from Peckett, Fox, Walker's successors. Carrying Peckett Works No. 528 it was named *George Jennings* after the pottery's founder and lasted for only nine years. In 1902 it was part-exchanged for a brand new 0-4-0 saddle tank locomotive also coming from Peckett. The name was transferred to the new engine Works No. 920, which was, presumably, more powerful to work up the hill to Parkstone station.

The South Western Pottery line emerges from the woods into Parkstone station goods yard across two diamond crossings. Peckett 0-4-0ST *George Jennings*, having left the mineral wagon (*right*) in the yard heads back to the pottery, 3rd July 1961.   *H.C. Casserley*

A delightful study of *George Jennings* and crew at Parkstone station goods yard. Having uncoupled the wagon brought up from the pottery they prepare to return light engine, 3rd July, 1961.   *H.C. Casserley*

The line from the pottery to Parkstone station goods yard remained in use until 1963 when it was also closed. This line climbed through woods to run close to the third and final pit where clay for the pottery was excavated; Baden Powell & St Peters School now stands here. The clay was transported to the pottery from this pit via a petrol/diesel-worked 2 ft narrow gauge line. Mechanical power came to the narrow gauge after World War I when the pottery obtained a war surplus petrol-engined Simplex locomotive which had served in France during hostilities. If indeed the original narrow gauge had ever been the suggested 51 inches, it must be assumed the change to 2 ft came at around this time, when new clay diggings at a second pit were opened. In 1930 the Simplex was joined by a second petrol locomotive, a Lister 4-wheeled machine, Works No. 3355. These two sufficed until 1948 when a battery locomotive was acquired; this was the least successful of the narrow gauge fleet and as such it was dumped in the mid-1950s after seeing little use. Its place was taken by Hibberd 'Planet' diesel No. 3790 of 1956.

No. 920 *George Jennings* was well employed during the early 1950s; the locomotive's daily work, Monday-Friday, involved shunting the pottery area as well as at least one trip to Parkstone station. However the pottery was in decline as more modern materials were taking over in the field of water and waste pipe manufacture. Eventually by 1961 the requirement to trundle up to Parkstone had dwindled to twice per week, usually Tuesdays and Fridays. Sometimes when the pottery engine and the British Railways daily pick-up freight happened to be at Parkstone at the same time, *George Jennings* would on the odd occasion, with the connivance of the BR crew, save them the work of an awkward shunt by moving the old tender containing the limescale brought over from the water softening plant at Bournemouth motive power depot. This

A 2 ft gauge Hibberd 'Planet' 4-wheeled diesel, Works No. 3790 of 1956, brings a load of clay to the pottery on 30th April, 1957.   *Austin Attewell (Photos from the Fifties)*

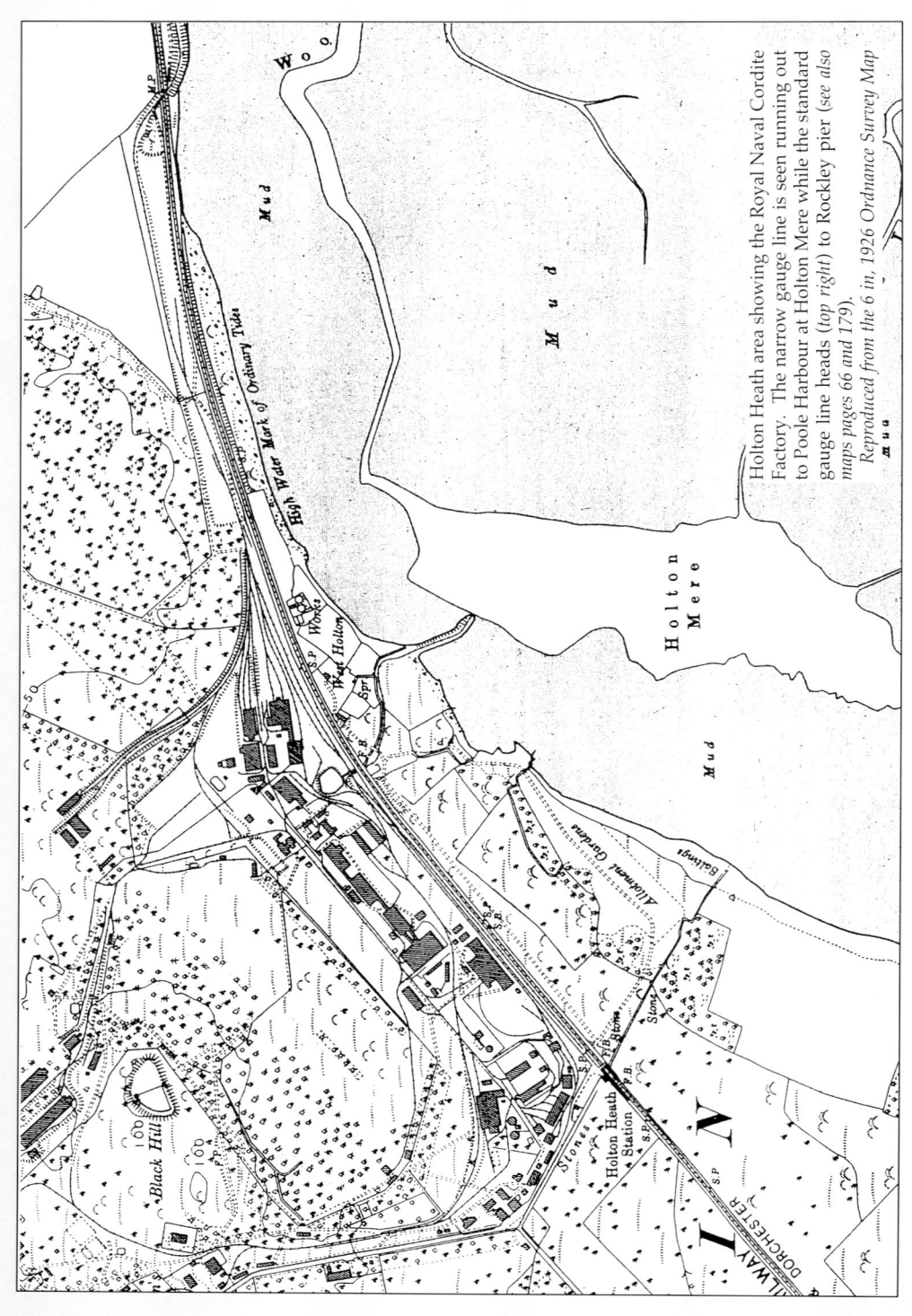

Holton Heath area showing the Royal Naval Cordite Factory. The narrow gauge line is seen running out to Poole Harbour at Holton Mere while the standard gauge line heads (*top right*) to Rockley pier (*see also maps pages 66 and 179*).
Reproduced from the 6 in, 1926 Ordnance Survey Map

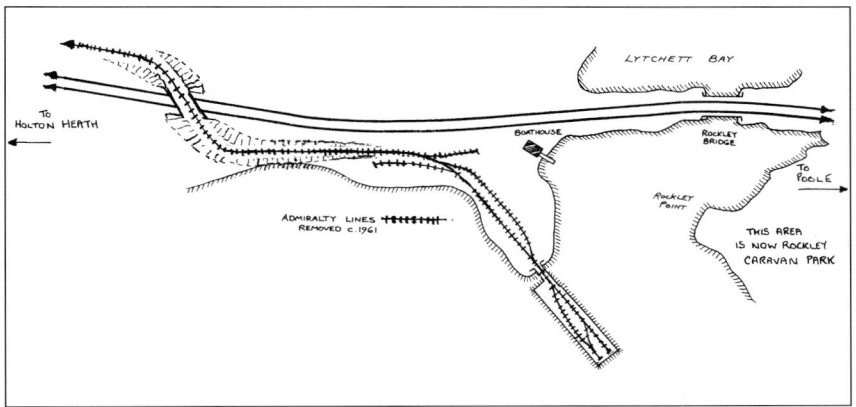

Track layout plan of the railways at Rockley (Rocklea) pier. *George Pryer*

The premises also had a substantial amount of internal standard gauge track totalling about five miles, the two locomotives (*see page 182*) were the final two engines used on site . The RNCF railway system and sidings were connected to the national railway system a few yards east of Holton Heath station.

This station was built initially for the factory workers and opened on 3rd April, 1916, and not until 1924 were the general public allowed to use it. The connection was into two reception sidings situated on the north side of the main Poole to Weymouth railway line, access being available from both up and down lines. However a second railway route for the cordite to leave the factory was also built; running parallel to the main railway line a standard gauge track was laid across the heath and through woodlands eastwards toward Hamworthy. On a gently rising gradient the line climbed to a height where it crossed the main railway line on a bridge, once over the top it descended to a point where it ran out to Rockley (Rocklea) jetty, about a mile distant from the factory. Built in 1915 at the same time as the cordite works, this jetty received its building materials via a temporary siding laid in from the down line of the LSWR main line; once work had been completed the siding was removed.

Cordite came down this Admiralty line for 22 years until 1938 to be transferred to sailing barges; it was then taken to the Navy Armament Depots at either Priddy's Hard, Gosport for Portsmouth Royal Naval Dockyard or to Upnor Castle on the River Medway in Kent for Chatham Royal Navy Docks. These sailing barges carried around a 100 tons payload, being usually towed by tug or powered craft between 'Stakes Buoy' and Rockley jetty as the channel which the Admiralty had arranged to be especially dredged for access to Rockley was too narrow to allow tacking against the wind. This towing practice lasted until steam-powered barges took over.

Motive power on the standard gauge part of the system was in the main steam until closure of the works in 1966 (although propellant production and major rail use had ceased in 1957). From 1938, during World War II the cordite went out by train on the main line to avoid German attacks on the barges.

A view looking east on the Waterloo to Weymouth main line, the former Southampton & Dorchester Railway. Crossing the line is the bridge carrying the RNCF line from the works to Rockley pier.   *R.W. Kidner*

The bridge which carried the RNCF line over the Waterloo-Weymouth main line remains *in situ*. Latterly partially plated over to allow vehicular access to Rockley Pier it is now used as an unofficial footpath leading to Poole Harbour as seen in this August 2006 view.   *Author*

Rockley pier viewed in 1976 looking south-west across Poole Harbour toward the Purbeck hills.
R.W. Kidner

Rockley pier looking inland, visible in the distance is the bunker of an RNCF Hunslet locomotive. At this time, May 1957, with nearly 20 years of disuse it was probably prudent not to allow the engine onto the rotting structure! *Hugh Davies (Photos from the Fifties)*

The last two locomotives to remain at the RNCF works were Bagnall 0-4-0ST Works No. 2596 built 1938 (Yard No. 1596) and Hunslet 0-6-0ST Works No. 1659 built in 1930 (Yard No 1627). Both are seen in this May 1957 view.   *Hugh Davies (Photos from the Fifties)*

In 1957 with the run down of the Holton Heath Cordite Factory under way, railway enthusiasts were allowed to visit the internal railway system. In this photograph the Hunslet 0-6-0ST is at the head of a 'special' train to Rockley pier. The engine once worked in Palestine at Haifa Harbour and was returned to England and rebuilt in 1938 before coming to the works in the same year.   *Hugh Davies (Photos from the Fifties)*

The works' remote location dictated a dedicated train service which reached its peak in World War II when the factory worked continuously on three eight-hour shifts. The service brought in personnel from Swanage, Wareham, Poole, Bournemouth and Christchurch and utilised an old South Eastern & Chatham Railway 'Birdcage' coach set. The daytime working conveyed mostly young ladies to the factory and became known as the 'Glamour Puffer' due to their youthful good looks. On 21st March, 1941 the 5.19 pm Holton Heath to Christchurch was caught in a sneak attack on Rockley Bridge by a lone German bomber. As the train approached the bridge six bombs fell close to the bridge and train, blowing out carriage windows, etc.; luckily no one was killed and only minor injuries occurred.

The Hawthorn, Leslie locomotives *Clausentum* and *Ironside* referred to earlier were loaned to the site in 1915 by the LSWR. They were used for construction traffic and it is suspected that in 1916 *Ironside* remained on short term loan as works shunter in company with the S&D 0-4-0T No. 26A, ex-Poole West Bay military sidings referred to earlier, until two RNCF locomotives arrived to take over shunting duties. These were Manning, Wardle 0-6-0 saddle tanks, Works No. 1228 of 1895 (RNCF No. 3), and Works No. 1620 of 1903 (RNCF No. 4). These engines lasted until 1925 when two 0-4-0ST locomotives came to the site, Avonside 0-4-0ST, Works No. 1976 built 1925, came new to the works taking the number RNCF No. 3 and replaced the original No. 3 which had been taken out of use in 1917. Hunslet 0-4-0ST, Works No. 3360 built 1918, became plain No. 16 and replaced RNCF No. 4 which went to Chatham Dockyard.

By coincidence both of these 1925 additions eventually came to work within the town of Poole. In 1935 the Hunslet was sold to work at Hamworthy, Ballast Quay becoming known as *Little Audrey*. In 1950 the 1925-built Avonside was transferred to shunt the railway-connected sidings of the 1941-built Creekmoor Royal Ordnance Factory (now part of the Siemens, Plessey, Sopers Lane, Poole site).

Finally in 1938 it was all change again when a brand new Bagnall 0-4-0ST 2596/38 arrived, this carried a cast number plate No. 1596. In the same year a Hunslet 0-6-0ST, Works No. 1659 originally of 1930 but rebuilt in 1938, arrived at the premises to be numbered 1627 and named *Reliance*. This locomotive had seen service in Palestine at Haifa Harbour.

They were joined by a new 1938-built 28 hp Baguley petrol railcar and in 1941 by a 4-wheeled Ruston, Hornsby diesel (Works No. 207103); both of these internal combustion additions had left the site by 1953. This left the two steam engines on site until 1961 when most rail traffic ceased; the Bagnall was then scrapped, *Reliance* seeing limited use on the odd stores train until it too went to the scrapman in 1966.

To stand opposite the site of Rockley Jetty at Rockley Point which is now a holiday camp, and watch the yachts and sailboards skimming across the water surface it is difficult to imagine that this most deadly of cargoes was once loaded there.

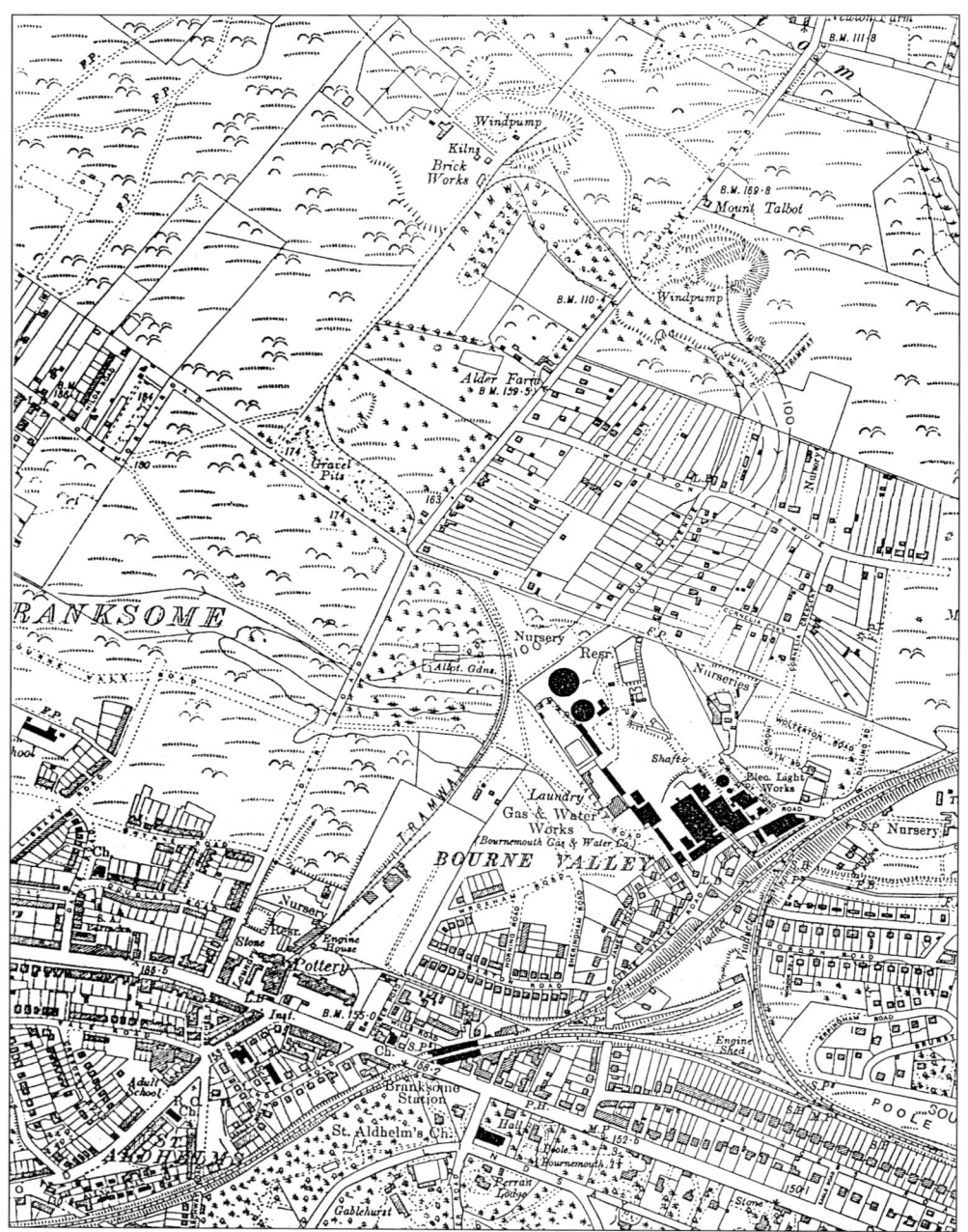

A map of the Branksome area of Poole includes Sharp, Jones & Co. railway 'The Bourne Valley Tramway'. *Reproduced from the 6 in., 1926 Ordnance Survey Map*

An inland diversion, The Bourne Valley Railway

Initially details of the following railway were omitted as it did not connect to the harbour, however, several persons suggested it be included; in truth they were correct to make the suggestion as the line was quite substantial, therefore the following notes will complete the scene regarding Poole's industrial rail links.

Sharp, Jones & Co. Ltd opened Bourne Valley Pottery in 1853 on the site now known as Redlands Trading Estate situated at the junction of Bournemouth Road, Ashley Road and Poole Road. This company in similar vein to South Western Pottery made bricks and earthenware pipes for underground water and sewage use. Initially their clay supply was dug locally in the vicinity of the pottery, in 1886, however, the company purchased additional clay land in the Bourne Bottom area situated between what is today Alder Crescent and Bloxworth Road. It was decided to bring this clay to the pottery by rail and to that end the pottery company constructed a standard gauge line of about 1¼ miles in length. Originally a dozen horses hauled the clay to the pottery over some quite fierce gradients. At a later date this line was connected to the main LSWR line near Branksome station. In June 1889 the company took delivery of a brand new steam locomotive built in Leeds by Hudswell, Clarke & Co. (Works No. 336). It was named *Pioneer* and was very similar in design to the locomotive *Pioneer* owned by the LSWR that operated on the Poole Quay line. This *Pioneer* was again an 0-4-0 saddle tank, a type much favoured on industrial lightly-laid railway systems. She remained in use until 1914 when she was requisitioned by the Government to 'work at some sidings adjoining a military depot west of Poole, long since removed'.*

A second locomotive was delivered in 1915, this was from an order placed in 1914 with the Avonside Engine Co. Ltd of Bristol. The locomotive, Works No. 1701, was an 0-4-0 engine with side tanks and a fully-enclosed cab, it was named *Mars* and cost £879 (did the Government cover the cost?). *Pioneer* was at some stage returned, but in her absence a steam crane was hired to shunt the pottery area when *Mars* underwent a boiler repair, it is assumed clay haulage reverted to horse power during this period. Both locomotives when out at work were limited to one wagon load of clay weighing about nine tons due to the severe gradients along the route.

In the 1920s and 1930s as production at the pottery reached a peak both engines were in steam at the same time working many hours per day. In 1938 *Pioneer* received a new boiler plus, in place of the original copper firebox, a replacement made of steel. Traffic fell off during World War II and *Mars* was sold in 1942 to the British Periclase Co. Ltd of West Hartlepool, leaving *Pioneer* to soldier on until 1948, by when it had become uneconomical to work the clay pits. The line closed, and *Pioneer's* last duties during August and September of 1948 were to work the demolition trains as the track was lifted. With this job done, after nearly 60 years' faithful service she was cut up by local scrap merchant Charles Trent.

---

* This was the West Bay Military Sidings. The position of these sidings adjacent to Holes Bay thus give the Bourne Valley system via *Pioneer* a tenuous link to Poole Harbour. Later in June 1918 to the north of Poole town in the Sterte area two more military sidings were installed alongside the Poole to Broadstone line and connected to the main line close to Holes Bay Junction. One report suggests *Pioneer* then saw use at this location, known as Longfleet Sidings, to shunt at the site which remained under military control until 1920. The sidings then passed into industrial ownership and *Pioneer* was returned to Sharp, Jones Ltd.

Sharp, Jones & Co. 0-4-0ST locomotive bought new in 1889 from Hudswell, Clarke (Works No. 336) is seen in the pottery yard *circa* 1930. Note the large patch on the smokebox.

R.C. Riley/Transport Treasury Collection

A view along the course of the Bourne Valley Railway in 1906 looking toward the clay pits. Local carrier W. Scott is taking a short cut across the line.

Forsey Collection/Poole Historical Trust/Poole Museums

Avonside 0-4-0T Works No. 1701 *Mars* built in 1915 came to the pottery system in that year and is seen at work on the line near the Alder Road crossing in 1925. Driver Sammy Speck is in charge of the locomotive and its load of one clay wagon.　　*Poole Museums*

The connection to British Railways at Branksome stayed in use until 1970, this was in part double track and crossed Cromer Road on the level. BR engines, normally one of Bournemouth's 'B4' class 0-4-0Ts, worked traffic into and out of the pottery although sometimes a Midland '2P' 4-4-0 from Branksome S&D shed was used. Internally the works sidings also remained and from 1948 a road tractor replaced *Pioneer* to shunt them. In the latter years the pottery under the ownership of Redland Pipes - successors to Sharp, Jones - forsook clay, turning to more 'modern' materials, some notable pottery products being large diameter concrete and 'spun' glass fibre pipes.

The line or tramway out of the pottery ran down a very steep incline of 1 in 22 to the bottom of the valley where Yarmouth Road now runs; it made a level crossing of Sheringham Road (when it was built in later years), today a large gap between houses marks its former course. The line then climbed on a long curve up the other side of the valley and crossed a rough track which is now Alder Road, the crossing point being where the junction with Herbert Avenue is now sited. The line continued parallel to Alder Road to reach a rail junction, straight ahead after crossing the Bourne stream lay the original rail-served clay pit (closed 1920). The other track from the junction ran eastwards following the Bourne stream and crossed Alder Road once again before ending at clay pits near Mount Talbot; traces of these pits can be seen at the end of the present day Sharp Road.

Two scenes taken in 2006 depicting the sorry state of the Hamworthy Goods branch.
Above: A view looking toward New Quay show the tracks disappearing under a sea of weeds. There has not been a visit by a weed control train for a number of years.
Right: The former goods yard is now part of a boat builder's car park, however some rails of the access siding to Railway Wharf are still *in situ*.   *(Both) Author*

Chapter Seven

The Present Day

In 1999 a foray around the area to discover what remained of the railway connections to Poole Harbour for the first edition of this publication revealed that very little was still in existence. Another foray and survey in 2006 to facilitate this edition has revealed, as could be expected, that certain subtle changes have taken place in the intervening years. On the Isle of Purbeck evidence of narrow gauge lines is varied. Of Pike's system, some evidence of the inland trackbed remains around Furzebrook and Creech. In the Creech area near remnants of trackbed some former rails have found further use as fence posts, whilst other short lengths are dumped in the tangled undergrowth. Part of the line from Furzebrook to the River Frome at Ridge has, in places, been turned into a footpath. At Ridge itself the former area where clay was transhipped onto barges for onward movement to Poole Quay is now a private boat yard. However adjacent to the public highway the former engine shed, now a listed building, still stands. But the most tangible relic of Pike Brothers' narrow gauge railway is now back on Purbeck. This is the second locomotive built for the line, the delightful 0-6-0WT locomotive named *Secundus*, which was built in 1874 by Bellis & Seekings, Birmingham. *Secundus* is on indefinite loan to the Swanage Railway from the Birmingham Museum of Science & Industry. At present *Secundus* is installed in a museum created in the former goods shed at Corfe Castle station; eventually the locomotive will be transferred to a purpose-built museum at Norden (*see below*).

Moving on to the Fayle's system almost all of the line across the heath to Goathorn on the shore of Poole harbour has been lost back to nature. However, in places earthworks as indentations in the ground indicate its former route where it traversed shallow cuttings. A once rarely-viewed relic of this system, the skew bridge which carried its rails over the former LSWR Swanage branch is now probably the most well-known feature of Fayle's railway. The bridge located at Norden is seen and much photographed by visitors to the Swanage Railway as they point their cameras at trains arriving into the Norden park-and-ride station from Swanage. This bridge will be incorporated into a working museum dedicated to the Purbeck clay mining industry which is being constructed at Norden by the Purbeck Mineral and Mining Musem Group.

On Brownsea Island there are no signs that a railway ever existed at all, similarly all traces of Salterns Pier and the railway to it have also long since disappeared. Rockley Jetty has suffered the same fate, although at low water one or two rotting stumps of support legs are just visible. Strangely, after nearly 50 years' disuse the bridge which carried the RNCF track to the jetty from Holton Heath cordite works still spans the main railway line to Weymouth. The Bourne Valley Railway is not completely lost, around 100 yards of trackbed remain parallel to Northmere Road and is easily visible and accessible. Also a very short section of the 1 in 22 incline from the pottery site down into Bourne Valley is still extant, but now incorporated into the rear garden of one of the

A view of the modern order on Waterloo-Weymouth passenger services since the demise in February 2007 of the much loved, more comfortable class '442' 'Wessex Electrics'. A German-built Siemens 'Desiro' unit No. 444008 works the 12.48 Weymouth to Waterloo service at Poole station on 29th April, 2007.   *Author*

Poole station buildings are visible in this view of Freightliner's class' 66' No. 66555 passing with the Wool to Neasden sand train on 2nd April, 2007. This was one of the first occasions that brand new wagons were in use.   *Author*

properties in Sheringham Road. Similarly, on the other side of the valley where the line climbed up to cross Alder Road, part of the trackbed is still extant and visible from a footpath which connects Holt Road and Stalham Road. It is also just visible in a couple of private gardens in this vicinity.

The Poole Quay Tramway is just a memory to a few old 'Pooleites', while across at Hamworthy a few rails are embedded in the concrete of J.T. Sydenham Timber Co.'s yard. However, a proposed redevelopment of this site will no doubt see the removal of these remnants for scrap. The rails that gave access to J.T. Sydenham's Waterloo Wharf ran through Carter's Pottery, Shapwick Road site but they were ripped up in 1994 when the premises were demolished. Rails of the 1926 extension to 'Siding No. 1' in the former Railway Wharf, once visible from Poole bridge, are now buried under buildings of a new Sunseeker boat yard. Rails on Ballast Quay, once the haunt of *Bonnie Prince Charlie* and *Western Pride*, disappeared in the 1980s. But it is here on the Hamworthy peninsular, where, in 1847, trains first arrived in Poole that some rails remain in place and these tracks still continue on to New Quay to give commercial access to Poole Harbour waters.

Unfortunately the Hamworthy branch is now seeing lower levels of traffic than in 1992 when the threat of closure was imminent. Luckily for the branch, stone trains from the Mendips continue to run bringing revenue to the branch, but sadly at the time of writing (September 2006) there are no transfers of cargo/freight from ship to rail or vice versa at this location. A recent announcement by PHC has indicated that a major steel handling company will cease using Poole as a steel import base, and steel consignments will go direct from European steel production points to UK destinations by rail via the Channel Tunnel. While good news in general for the rail over road lobby, it is bad news for the Port of Poole and any chance of steel imports through Poole continuing onwards by rail via the Hamworthy branch.

A previous chapter has documented the rise, fall and eventual demise of import/export freight over the Hamworthy line, it can only be hoped that the future will see an upturn in the fortunes of the line. One good omen is that Poole Borough Council Transportation Department has made mention of the line, a major redevelopment scheme for the Hamworthy peninsular includes retention of the Hamworthy branch, so that at least provides a small crumb of comfort.

A life of 110 years carrying just freight traffic was passed in 2006, and the year 2007 heralds 160 years existence of the Hamworthy line. Hamworthy Goods station is where rail passengers for Poole first arrived, thus it would be a shame to lose yet another part of Poole's heritage should the line close. The fact that Hamworthy Goods station marks the spot where standard gauge rails were first laid in the County of Dorset probably does not rank highly in the greater scheme of things, but to lose this line for future commercial use at this stage in its life would be a tragedy.

We have to hope that the downturn in freight transfers from ship to rail and vice versa are just a temporary hiccough and will not lead to the end of 'Rails to Poole Harbour'.

Poole Park Miniature Railway 4-4-2 *Vanguard* heads a full load of passengers around the circuit in August 1954.   *Ivo Peters courtesy of Julian Peters*

On the same day *Vanguard* comes off the 'new' bridge crossing the fresh water lake within Poole Park. The original bridge at this point was a casualty of the Luftwaffe in World War II!   *Ivo Peters courtesy of Julian Peters*

Appendix One

Poole Park Miniature Railway

Earlier in the text mention has been made of the 1874 railway extension from Poole to Bournemouth West bisecting Parkstone Bay within Poole harbour on a causeway. As stated, subsequent development of the area during 1890 into Poole Park saw the enclosed water being turned into a boating lake.

During the construction of the park the eastern end of this lake was further bisected by a road causeway giving rise to a second smaller lake. Over the years due to inflowing streams and springs the water in this smaller lake gradually became fresh, allowing it to be turned into an ornamental lake complete with carp and other fresh water fish and wildlife. In 1949 a concern by the name of Southern Miniature Railways constructed a 10¼ in. gauge railway around its circumference. For over 50 years trains have plied around its ½ mile-long circuit giving rides and pleasure to countless youngsters and even the not so young as grandfathers, etc. are enticed into a ride on the train.

In early days motive power was a 4-4-2 steam locomotive bearing the number 1001 and the name *Vanguard*; she worked until 1969 when, partly due to rising coal costs, it was decided to replace steam with a 'diesel'. *Vanguard* was subsequently sold; it is thought that the locomotive still exists in private ownership.

She was replaced by a petrol-engined machine numbered D107 bearing a resemblance to a class '52' 'Western' diesel, this in turn being replaced by an 'HST' power car outline locomotive. Under the auspices of a new owner from 1991 to 1998 steam returned to the line in the shape of a freelance 0-6-0ST *Arthur* based on a National Coal Board engine, sadly this engine was sold which left the 'HST' as motive power. The miniature railway was sold again in 2005 and the 'HST' has been joined by a steam-outline 0-6-0 diesel locomotive.

As this line runs along the causeway between the two lakes with the sea water boating lake section of Parkstone Bay on its right-hand side, it can be argued that in its own way the Poole Park Miniature Railway does give a railway connection to Poole Harbour!

The current motive power on the line photographed in 1990 is this Bo-Co HST power car-outline locomotive. *Author*

Appendix Two

Private Sidings in Poole

The following table lists all known industrial/private companies within Poole which at some time had a private siding/s or connection to the London and South Western Railway, Southern Railway and/or its successor British Railways.

Company	Status	Location and Notes
Branksome Gas Works (Bourne Valley)	Siding	Branksome Adjacent main line, extending from Bourne Valley viaduct over Coy Pond Road bridge, for coal deliveries down chutes and via a short 'tramway' to premises in Bourne Valley. Siding removed 1965.
Sharp, Jones Ltd	Main line connection	Branksome Access to works sidings and internal rail system inbound coal/coke, pipes out.
South Western Pottery	Access to main line	Parkstone Internal rail system, connected to goods yard sidings: inbound; coal/coke, pipes: outbound; pipes.
Poole Gas Works (Bournemouth Gas & Water Co.)	Main line connection	Poole Internal siding system, stores and some coal inbound plus from *c.* 1965 Naptha spirit for a new plant. Tar and coke out, works and system closed 1973. Also narrow gauge system serving retorts etc. Standard gauge locomotives No. 1 4wPM Hudsons, Leeds new 1924, scrapped 1946, No. 2 4wDM Hibberd 'Planet' 2054/38, No. 3 4wDM Ruston & Hornsby 242867/46.*
British Government (Military)	Sidings	Poole Temporary sidings 1915-1920 West Quay Road area.
Blue Circle Cement Co.	Main line access	Poole Cement distribution Plant constructed in Poole station goods yard *c.* 1960. Inbound, cement powder in 'PRESFLO' wagons from Westbury for local distribution. Closed *c.* 1985.
Hill Richards Ltd. & Waller Housing Corp.	Sidings	Sterte Situated on land along side Stanley Green Road now occupied by industrial units. Inbound building materials, including shingle from West Bay near Bridport. Site used by Hill Richards from mid-1920. Originally in use as two Military sidings with a spur to a works building, laid in 1918 known as 'Longfleet sidings', sidings out of use by 1922. Part of the site included a concrete works in later years known as W.S. Try Ltd. Evidence exists suggesting this works originally

* 4wPM/4wDM = 4-wheeled petrol/diesel-mechanical.

Peckett 0-4-0ST Works No. 2012/41, one time resident shunter at Creekmoor ROF has survived and is preserved, it is seen here at Cadeby Rectory in 2005 before movement to the Hollycombe Steam Museum.   *Martin Ellis*

Company	Status	Location and Notes
Hill Richards Ltd. (cont.)		received sand from the Hatch Pond area (about a mile distant) via a short-lived narrow gauge tramway.
Ministry of Supply (Creekmoor Royal Ordnance Factory)	Main line connection	Creekmoor Small internal railway system serving armaments factory built in 1941 at Sopers Lane, internal motive power Peckett 0-4-0ST 2012/41 and from 1950 Avonside 0-4-0ST 1976/25. Site disused by 1959, now owned by Siemens, Plessey and Barclays International. Inbound raw materials? (metal), out weapons/munitions.
Sykes' Pottery	Siding	Creekmoor Connected to main line at Creekmoor Halt. Site now part of Creekmoor Industrial Estate. Inbound coal/coke, outbound pipes, bricks etc. Out of use by 1966. The Pottery also had an extensive 2 ft gauge system bringing sand from pits to works via a tunnel under a public road (Cabot Lane). Eight 4-wheeled diesel mechanical locomotives worked the system.
Doulton & Co.	Siding	Creekmoor/Broadstone Adjacent, and connected to the main line between Hamworthy and Broadstone (Castleman's Corkscrew). Laid as late as 1962 to serve a new clay pit. Main line closed 1966, access maintained from Broadstone as a 'long siding' finally taken out of use 1973. Outbound, clay.
Lytchett Brickworks (later known as Upton Brickworks)	Siding	Upton Opened 1890 adjacent and connected to the main line between Hamworthy and Broadstone (Castleman's Corkscrew). Siding on west side of line (just outside borough boundary).

Class '04' diesel shunter No. D2274 works a branch trip freight near Hamworthy Junction in 1960. On the skyline is a training building within the Royal Marine base, the line extreme left is the siding into Kinson Pottery. *Author's Collection*

Company	Status	Location and Notes
Lytchett Brickworks (cont.)	Siding	Removed 1966 on closure of the line. Works also served by internal 2 ft gauge line worked by 12 diesel/petrol locomotives. Inbound coal/coke, outbound clay and bricks.
Dorset Clay Products	Siding	Upton Opened 1948 adjacent and connected to the main line between Hamworthy and Broadstone (Castleman's Corkscrew). Siding on east side of line (just outside borough boundary) removed 1966 on closure of the line. Outbound clay.
Kinson Pottery Ltd	Siding	Hamworthy Access to main line via connection at Hamworthy Jn station, in use from 1890s finally lifted 1971. Inbound coal/coke, out bricks/tiles. Siding used to store explosives wagons etc. during World War I.
Associated Portland Cement Marketing Co.	Sidings	Hamworthy Purpose-built cement (powder) receiving terminal constructed and opened in 1975 and closed by 1988, replaced old depot at Hamworthy New Quay.
Air Ministry (later British Pipeline Agency)	Sidings	Hamworthy (Lake) Two sidings constructed off the Hamworthy Goods branch, laid in 1938 removed *c.* 1970. Inbound aviation fuel and petrol, piped to fuel storage facility off Lake Drive for naval flying boat use during World War II. Later as a strategic reserve until *c.* 1980.
Doulton & Co.	Siding	Hamworthy (Lake) Siding off Hamworthy Goods branch opened 1929, closed 1964, lifted 1966. Outbound clay. This site off Lake Road used as landfill tip by Brooks Ltd, builders, in the 1970s and is now a housing estate.

The Associated Portland Cement Co. terminal at the Dawkins Road Industrial Estate adjacent to the Hamworthy Goods line. The depot was built and opened in 1975 when the company moved from their former premises on New Quay, Hamworthy (*see photograph on title page*). By the time of this photograph (May 1988) the site had been disused for a year, the sidings were later removed and the silos demolished in 1999. The site is now used as a stockpile point for stone from the Mendips and as a loading point for fragmentised scrap steel.　　　*Author*

Company	*Status*	*Location and Notes*
Admiralty	Siding	Hamworthy (Lake) Siding off Hamworthy Goods branch. Former up line relaid 1916 to serve shipyard. Inbound raw materials and equipment.
J.R. Smith Steel Stockholders	Siding	Hamworthy (Lake) Siding off Hamworthy Goods branch addition to long siding into former Admiralty shipyard, later flying boat base. Inbound structural steelwork, i.e. girders. Formerly J. Smith's Ironworks and general dealer.
Carter's Pottery	Siding	*See main text.*
J.T. Sydenham	Siding	*See main text.*
Hamworthy Wharf & Coal Co.	Sidings	*See main text.* Later J.R. Wood and Corralls.
James Bros Ltd Structural Engineers and steel stock holders	Goods Yard	Hamworthy Originally served by a siding, by the 1960s this company used the old goods loading platform at Hamworthy Goods station to receive structural steel, i.e. girders.
Poole Harbour Commissioners	Sidings	Formerly part of the Hamworthy Goods branch below mileage point 117.67, extending on to New Quay. Control assumed from BR/Railtrack as and from May 1992 to present day.

Poole Freight Workings
in 1960

Up direction (Monday-Friday)

6.08/6.39 am (calling), Salisbury-Bournemouth East yard
6.42/7.10 am (calling), Bath-Bournemouth West
8.17 am arr. ex-Evercreech
9.27 am dep. to Bournemouth East yard
11.43 am arr. ex-Evercreech
12.27 pm arr. ex-Broadstone
12.58 pm arr. ex-Eastleigh via Wimborne
12.58 pm dep. to Bournemouth East yard
1.54/2.35 pm (calling), Hamworthy Junction-Bournemouth East yard
6.32 pm arr. ex-Hamworthy Junction
6.58/7.55 pm (calling), Corfe Castle-Bournemouth East yard
8.15/9.15 pm (calling), Dorchester-Nine Elms (Dorset Goods)
11.30 pm dep. to Eastleigh

Down direction (Monday-Friday)

1.06/1.30 am (calling), Eastleigh-Dorchester
3.39 am arr. ex-Bournemouth East yard
4.23/5.05 am (calling), Nine Elms-Weymouth (Dorset Goods)
6.09 am dep. to Swanage
8.50 am dep. to Brockenhurst via Wimborne
9.05 am dep. to Hamworthy Junction
10.57 am dep. to Broadstone
1.00 pm arr. ex-Bournemouth East yard
1.27 pm dep. to Hamworthy Junction
3.05 pm dep. to Templecombe
4.29 pm arr. from Bournemouth East yard
5.25/6.08 pm (calling), Bournemouth East yard-Dorchester
6.28/6.48 pm (calling), Bournemouth East yard-Dorchester *
   (Did not run if Redbridge ran, see below)
8.17/8.20 pm (calling), Redbridge-Dorchester - as required see above
8.10 pm dep. to Bath

* Conditional Friday/Saturday excepted relief.

Appendix Four

The Creekmoor Light Railway

The map on Page 10 shows the siding (annotated 11) off the main line serving Upton Brickworks formerly known as Lytchett Brickworks. This works had extensive clay and sand deposits on the adjacent heath which were brought part way to the works by a 2 ft gauge tramway and an aerial ropeway for the remainder of the distance. It appears that the tramway section went out of use around 1966, some three years before the brickworks finally closed in 1969. Around this time there were many golden opportunities for preserving items of railway and transport history as a lot of railway equipment was becoming redundant. In 1967 whilst working adjacent to Upton Brickworks local enthusiast Trevor Waterman was presented with one such opportunity when he learnt of the imminent disposal of the narrow gauge system and its equipment. Having purchased two of the 2 ft gauge locomotives, 15 brick-carrying wagons and a quantity of rails, pins and points, Mr Waterman then enlisted the assistance of six fellow railway enthusiasts to build a railway.

Subsequent construction was undertaken around a mile distant from the brickworks site on Mr Waterman's smallholding at Creekmoor Lane near Broadstone and thus the 'Creekmoor Light Railway' (CLR) was born. A three-road sleeper-built engine shed/depot was built to house the stock and the interior of the shed was adorned with enamel targets and running-in nameboards from the adjacent BR Creekmoor Halt (closed 1966). Windows from the halt were salvaged and re-used as well. The CLR consisted of a main line which ran for just over a quarter of a mile, from the depot it crossed the access road to the smallholding then into and around a large pasture field. Curving around some oak trees the rails climbed sharply through a gate and up to a loop complete with two sidings that overlooked the BR line to Broadstone, Wimborne and Ringwood, which by 1967 was freight only. In 1971 to help finance the purchase of a steam locomotive a bid was presented to British Railways stores department. The bid of 10s. 6d. (52½p) was accepted and was for the purchase of redundant signalling equipment in the Broadstone station area. Over three weekends a platelayers' trolley loaded with oxy-acetylene equipment was wheeled about a mile up the 1 in 75 gradient of the British Railways line from Creekmoor Halt to Broadstone station. Signal posts, signals, pulleys, stools and cast-iron signs from the station and goods yard area were then removed and loaded onto the trolley. Back at the CLR the signalling gear was sorted for scrap/sale or for further use on the railway. Several signals and ground signals (dummies) were used, the whole line was track circuited complete with track diagram located in a signal box at 'Pines Summit' overlooking the BR line. This home made signal box complete with lever frame came from former 'Castleman's Corkscrew' Uddens Crossing box east of Wimborne. Also the former ticket office from Creekmoor Halt was dismantled and rebuilt on the CLR as a 'gate box' on the access road (*see photograph page 49*). Although primarily built as a preservation scheme, it had been intended to use the line for commercial purposes and move some of the farm/smallholding produce over the line. The locomotive fleet comprised:

Samson	4wDM built by Hibberd, Works No. 1887 of 1934.*
Delilah	4wDM built by Motor Rail, Works No. 9778 of 1953.* A rolling chassis remained in stripped down condition.
Brunel	4wDM built by Ruston & Hornsby, Works No. 179880 of 1936. From L.W. Vass (dealer) Bedfordshire, December 1969.
Druid or *David*	4wDM built by Motor Rail, Works No. 8644 of 1941 of 1936. Acquired from Pollock & Brown, Southampton in 1971.

199

A triple-header on the Creekmoor Light Railway, the Orenstein & Koppel 0-6-0T steam locomotive *Fojo* leads two of the CLR diesels on a works train.
Tony Legg

Fojo	0-6-0WT built by Orenstein & Koppel, Berlin, Works No. 9239 of 1921. From Empressa Carbonifera de Douro, Portugal via Alan Keef, Oxfordshire in August 1972.

4wDM 4-wheeled diesel-mechanical.   * From Upton Brickworks.

Rolling stock comprised a 14 ft-long, 12-seat passenger coach built at the CLR using two bogies taken from former brick-carrying wagons and adapted to suit. Also built on site using materials and parts from Upton Brickworks rolling stock were a 16 ft rail carrier, two drop-sided wagons, and a sizeable tool van. Any items of former brickworks stock not used for building the new stock became part of CLR fleet and this included sand skips.

The Creekmoor Light Railway existed from October 1968 to May 1973 when the smallholding along with seven other similar adjacent properties were sold for redevelopment, Creekmoor housing estate now covers the site. So ended Poole's short and frenetic entry into the preservation scene; as such *Fojo* was the town's last working steam locomotive. It was not quite the end of the story as the railway was moved some 30 miles west across Dorset to Crockway Farm near Frampton. The new site was visible from the ex-GWR line between Dorchester South and Maiden Newton and attracted 'friendly toots' from passing main line trains. However, the narrow gauge line became dormant as the original volunteer work force turned their attention and labour to resurrecting what was then the recently closed Swanage branch.

In 1977 the whole of the narrow gauge stock, signs and memorabilia was sold by auction and scattered far and wide. The steam locomotive *Fojo* moved to Hertfordshire where it was renamed *Nantmor*. Subsequently the locomotive was acquired by an enthusiast in Surrey and is currently believed to be awaiting overhaul at the Boston Lodge works of the Festiniog Railway, Porthmadog. Of the diesels, there is no trace of *Delilah*, however, *Brunel* now resides at Lynton, Devon, *Sampson* went to Colne, Lancashire, while *Druid* can be found in Leeds, Yorkshire.

In April 1970, Ruston & Hornsby 4-wheeled diesel *Brunel* is seen with a partially-built passenger coach.   *Tony Legg*

Appendix Five

Stephen Lewin and the Poole Foundry

If asked to name a company which built industrial steam locomotives, most persons interested in that type of machine would no doubt suggest companies like Bagnall of Stafford, Hudswell, Clarke of Leeds or Peckett of Bristol. The name Lewin of Poole would not rank high on the list of industrial railway locomotive builders, but nevertheless such engines were indeed constructed in the town of Poole. The recent construction of two replica locomotives named *Ant* and *Bee* for the Great Laxey Mine Museum on the Isle of Man brought the name of Stephen Lewin into the public eye once again. The original *Ant* and *Bee* were diminutive 0-4-0 well tanks built by Lewin in 1877 to a gauge of 1 ft 7 in. for the Great Laxey Mining Co. Ltd, They were not, however, the first locomotives to be constructed in Poole. Exactly when the first locomotive left Stephen Lewin's Poole Foundry is lost in the mist of time as no substantial records remain, but it does seem most probable that 1868 was the year in which a railway locomotive first emerged from the foundry.

Poole Foundry's origins went back to *circa* 1841 when William Pearce, a Poole ironmonger, purchased land to expanded his business by building agricultural equipment. The original site was twice expanded and the foundry was well into production by 1850. In 1863 Pearce sold the business to William Wilkinson and Stephen Lewin, however, Wilkinson left the company under a cloud of controversy in 1868 and after his departure certain financial irregularities were discovered in the foundry's books. Stephen Lewin continued alone and business increased by leaps and bounds, not only was the foundry building agricultural machinery but it also ventured into the field of building stationary steam boilers, portable steam engines and steam yachts. By 1874 Poole Foundry was Poole's largest employer. In 1875 on the back of success and expanding trade Lewin was able to attract a large financial investment (£12,000, quite substantial for the time). What could have been the end for Lewin and Poole Foundry came in 1876 when a disastrous fire destroyed much of the premises. Although Poole Foundry survived it has been suggested that it never really recovered from the effects of the fire. A further blow to the business came in 1878 when its dynamic manager left to work for a rival concern, the Dorset Iron Foundry based in West Quay Road, Poole. After this, railway locomotive production ceased at Poole Foundry, one of the reasons being that this gentleman was responsible for designing the locomotives attributed to Lewin. A general decline in business for both the foundry and timber importation, in which Lewin was also involved, led to Stephen Lewin being declared bankrupt in 1884. That spelt the end for Poole Foundry, and its assets were auctioned off in September that year.

The Dorset Iron Foundry made a minor entry into locomotive production, building two engines for the Auckland Timber Co., New Zealand in 1881 and 1882. As no further locomotives were built by this company, 1882 must therefore mark the end of Poole's foray into the locomotive building industry. As mentioned above the first railway locomotive to be built in Poole was probably constructed between 1868 and 1870 and could well have been Fayle's 0-4-0 *Tiny* as an uncorroborated date of 1868 has been suggested for *Tiny*. A 1 ft 10 in. gauge 0-4-0WT, which in 1874 went to Middleton-in-Teesdale, County Durham to work for the London Lead Co., is the first locomotive for which there is a definite construction date. The year 1875 saw production of railway locomotives expand rapidly, the fact that Lewin engines were of simple but very sturdy construction was a great selling point.

Another factor in favour of Lewin engines was that in general all working parts were readily accessible and the locomotives were very easy to operate. Locomotives built in

A mystery locomotive viewed in the yard of Stephen Lewin's Poole Foundry. Obviously an 0-4-0T, it appears to be of standard gauge and 'cut down' for working within limited height clearances. The locomotive is awaiting movement to either Poole Quay or the railway station goods yard for onward shipment to its purchaser.   *Roger Smith Collection*

Poole went all over Britain, including as we have seen the Isle of Man, two others named *Hops* and *Malt* went further across the Irish Sea to Ireland working at the Guinness factory in Dublin. Records of locomotives built in Poole by Lewin are pretty sparse but the definitive work *Stephen Lewin and the Poole Foundry* by Russell Wear and Eric Lees lists 26 definite and six probable steam railway locomotives attributed to Poole Foundry.

Two of these locomotives lasted long enough to become well-known in railway enthusiasts' circles and, against all the odds for such a small production batch built way back in the 1870s, one actually survived long enough to be preserved. The first of these two minor celebrities is illustrated on page 162 and was the only Lewin engine to work locally in Dorset at Fayle & Co., Norden, Corfe Castle. Various dates have been suggested for her construction, i.e. 1863, 1870 or 1868, but the latter would appear to be the most feasible as this was the year Fayle's opened their first section of railway. Heavily rebuilt over the years, the engine, known as *Tiny*, lasted until 1948.

Conflicting dates for the construction of the surviving Lewin locomotive also abound, but in all probability she emerged in 1877. Sent north to County Durham, the locomotive, an 0-4-0WT, started work at Seaham Harbour Dock Co., then owned by the Marquis of Londonderry. The locomotive remained in use until the late 1960s, in the intervening years during overhauls she was also heavily rebuilt and altered. As well as receiving an enclosed cab (no doubt a necessity when working on the coast of the North Sea) the engine at first had side tanks fitted, but latterly was rebuilt as a saddle tank. However she still retained the 'Lewin look', i.e. solid cast driving wheels with holes rather than spokes, a circular connecting rod, angled cylinders and a dome placed well forward on the boiler.

This longevity took the engine into the age of preservation, therefore after some time out of use 1975 found the locomotive transferred to Beamish Open Air Museum. By 1978 the engine had been returned to her original condition as a well tank and was steamed until the 1980s. The locomotive is currently undergoing a full overhaul for an eventual return to steam (*see page 207*).

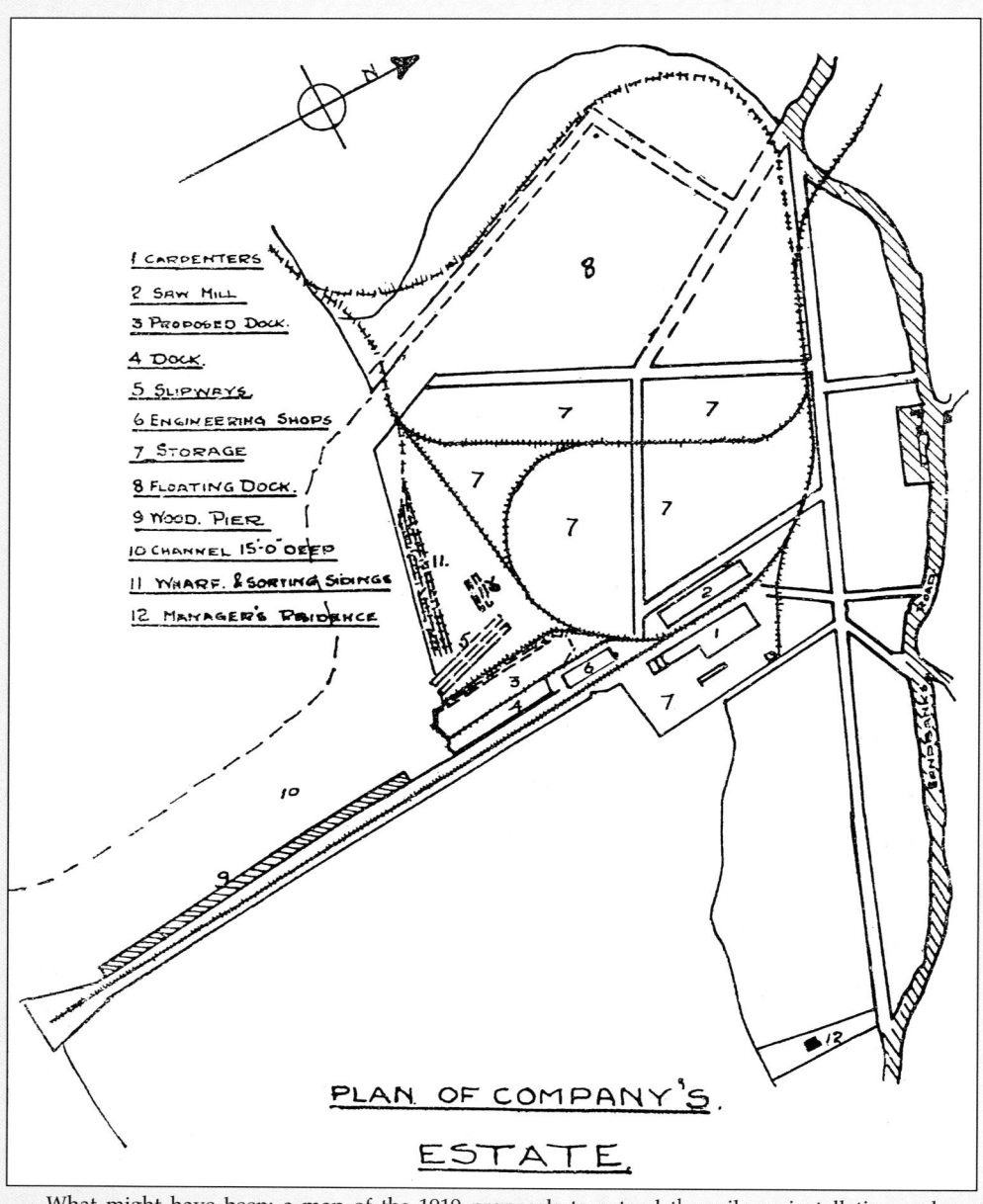

Key:
1 CARPENTERS
2 SAW MILL
3 PROPOSED DOCK.
4 DOCK.
5 SLIPWAYS
6 ENGINEERING SHOPS
7 STORAGE
8 FLOATING DOCK.
9 WOOD. PIER
10 CHANNEL 15'·0 DEEP
11 WHARF. & SORTING SIDINGS
12 MANAGER'S RESIDENCE

PLAN OF COMPANY'S ESTATE.

What might have been: a map of the 1919 proposals to extend the railway installation and expand the Salterns Pier area to turn it into a port/dock complex.

Appendix Six

What Might Have Been

Two recently discovered documents reveal proposals which if they had come to fruition would have made the history of 'Rails to Poole Harbour' a totally different proposition! The first document dated 1919 has revealed a plan to turn the area of Salterns into a 'port/dock' complex as a possible rival to the quays at Poole and Hamworthy. The document in question is a share Prospectus to raise £200,000 for a company called 'Salterns Limited, Shipbuilders, Repairers, Engineers & Transportation agents'. Directors of the company included W. Alban Richards owner/Director of the wagon repair company located at Salterns Pier, F. Van Raalte, then owner of Brownsea Island and H. Wragg, Director of Thomas Wragg i.e. South Western Pottery. Other prospective Directors were two shipowners, the reason for their involvement was due to the fact that Salterns Ltd intended, 'To purchase and convert the 320 ton tanker *Mountjoy* (owned by Burdens of Poole) when she will be continuously and profitably employed'. Plans also included building a new 500 ton ship for the granite trade! Whether this 'granite' was to be exported or imported was not stated.

A map accompanying the Prospectus showed projected sea connections to the Channel Islands and Cherbourg with an attached note: 'To French and Channel Island districts needing British Manufacturers'. A second map reproduced opposite reveals plans for a floating dock and extended sidings etc., one of which would have crossed the 'lock gate' of the floating dock. This plan never came to fruition, had it succeeded it is possible that the line from Parkstone station could have remained in use for some considerable time and maybe, just maybe, it might still be open; a tantalising thought?

The second 'find' was a map dated 1920, this map (*see overleaf*) showing a proposed redevelopment of both Poole and Hamworthy Quays. As this map was published just one year after the proposals for the Salterns Pier area it must be assumed to have been a 'knee jerk' reaction by the Port of Poole Authorities. The accompanying map shows just how massive a scheme was proposed. The fact that the north side wharf would have been about 1½ miles long and extended almost as far as Salterns Pier would suggest the Poole authorities were trying to intimidate the Salterns group.

A certain amount of infilling of Parkstone Bay would have afforded a connection to the LSWR main line at the bottom of Parkstone bank, whilst the Hamworthy branch would have gained a new connection to the south side wharves.

The modest Salterns Pier plan was the most feasible and could possibly have got off the ground, but it was probably scuppered by the Port of Poole scheme. This idea seems highly fanciful and in view of the shallow nature of Poole Harbour must have been a non-starter from the outset. The close proximity of Southampton as an established and successful deep water port would have impacted on any shipping movements. The Port of Poole plans were most probably a successful blocking move, as neither proposal was ever progressed.

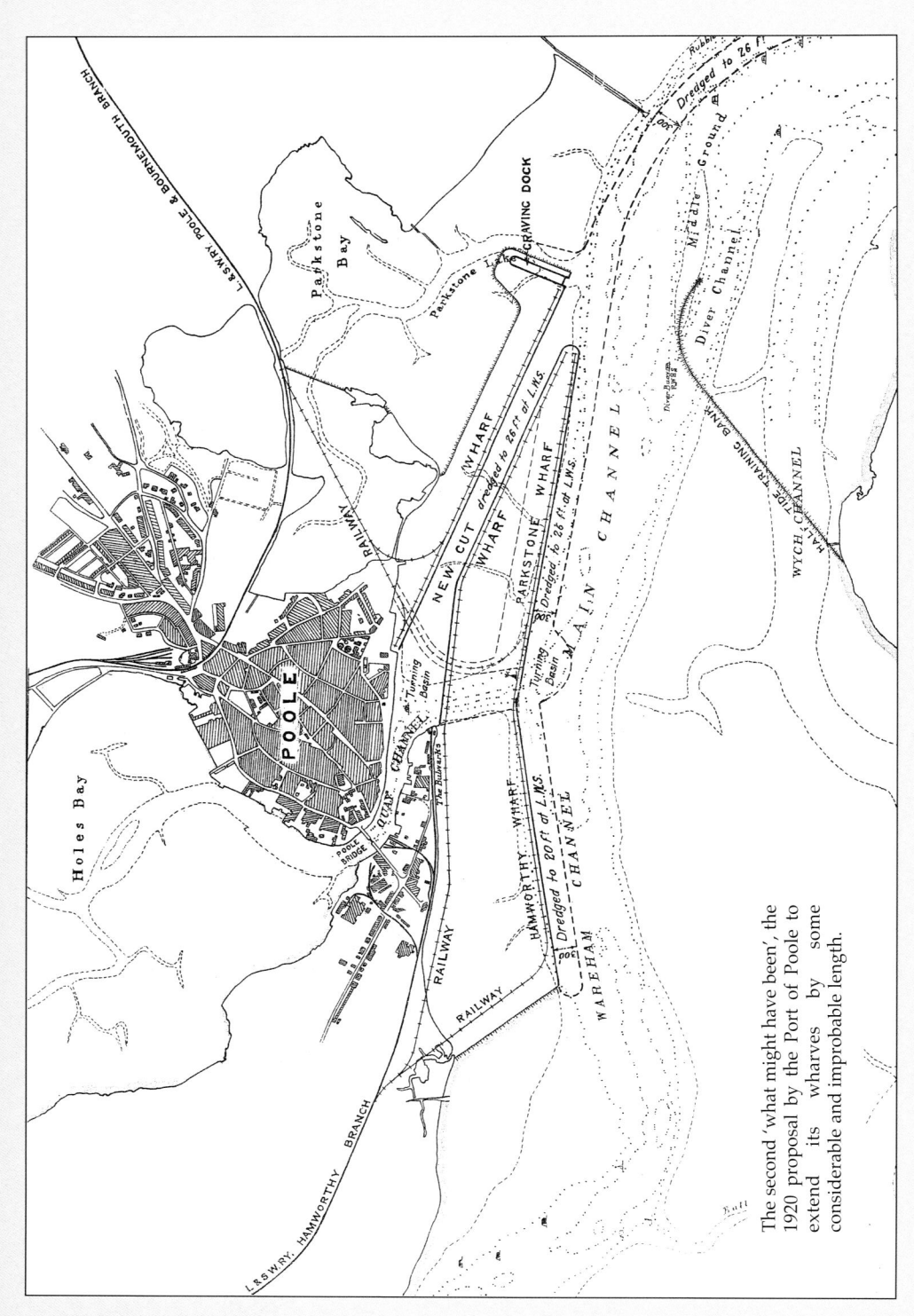

The second 'what might have been', the 1920 proposal by the Port of Poole to extend its wharves by some considerable and improbable length.

Bibliography

A History of Poole, C.N. Cullingford, Phillimore & Co., 1988.

Britain in Old Photographs - Poole, Ann Norbury, Alan Sutton Publishing, 1995.

Victorian Poole, John Hillier, Poole Historical Trust, 1985.

Ebb Tide at Poole, John Hillier, Poole Historical Trust, 1985.

Poole and World War II, Derek Beamish, Harold Bennett & John Hillier, Poole Historical Trust, 1980.

The Spirit of Poole, John Hillier & Martin Blyth, Poole Historical Trust, 1994.

Poole Town & Harbour, R. Blomfield, Dorset Publishing Co., 1989.

Cordite-Poole, M. Bowditch.

Poole, Ian Andrews, Phillimore & Co., 1994.

The B4 Dock Tanks, Peter Cooper, Kingfisher Railway Productions, 1988.

The Railways of Purbeck, R.W. Kidner, Oakwood Press, 1973.

London & South Western Locomotives, H.C. Casserley, Ian Allan, 1971.

Track Diagrams of the Southern Railway, A.V. Paul & G. Pryer, R.A. Cooke, 1980.

Railways of Dorset, J.H. Lucking, RCTS, 1968.

Port of Poole Official Handbook, 1954.

Industrial Locomotives of South Western England, Roger Hateley, Industrial Railway Society, 1977.

Stephen Lewin and the Poole Foundry, Russell Wear & Eric Lees, Industrial Railway Society & Industrial Locomotive Society, 1978.

MADE IN POOLE ... A remarkable survivor, the one and only Stephen Lewin engine to have escaped the scrap man. This 0-4-0WT Lewin engine spent its life in the North-East of England at Seaham Harbour, County Durham. Her light weight meant she was useful for work over lightly-laid tracks and around sharp curves in the docks area. This ensured longevity and survival into the 1970s, and eventual preservation. Now based at the Beamish Open Air Museum (where this picture is taken) she has been restored to near original condition.   *Ken Aveyard*

Index

Off the road at Poole. Class '442' unit No. 2421, which had suffered a seized traction motor the previous day, became derailed whilst being towed by electro-diesel No. 73109 on 6th July, 1992. The electro-diesel has departed the scene for Branksome depot with the two leading cars, as these had been fouling the main line. *Author*